THE RIDING TEACHER

THE
RIDING TEACHER

A BASIC GUIDE TO CORRECT METHODS
OF CLASSICAL INSTRUCTION

ALOIS PODHAJSKY
TRANSLATED BY EVA PODHAJSKY
DRAWINGS BY ANTON HAUG

 Harrap London

*Originally published in German under the
title "Reiten Lehren und Lernen"*

First published in Great Britain 1973
by GEORGE G. HARRAP & CO. LTD
182–184 High Holborn, London WC1V 7AX

Reprinted 1974; 1977

© *Nymphenburger Verlagshandlung GmbH., München* 1971
English translation © *Doubleday & Co., Inc.* 1972, 1973

ISBN 0 245 52041 4

Printed and bound in Great Britain by
REDWOOD BURN LIMITED
Trowbridge & Esher

This is to express my deep gratitude and love to my wife Eva who not only translated this book but also contributed to it by her observations as a spectator

CONTENTS

THE RIDING TEACHER

INTRODUCTION

For sixty years my life has been dedicated to the horse
and to riding, and it follows that in these six decades I have
had a chance to gain a relatively extensive and profound
knowledge of the subject. The experience I gathered from
my earliest childhood on was given time and opportunity to
develop and mature. Even in recent years it has been enlarged
by new contacts with the world of horsemanship. Corrobora-
tion of age-old principles and understanding of new aspects
have led to a conception of the subject which I hope may be
called well balanced and comprehensive.

It is with great pleasure that I would like to pass on my
experiences and my advice to the young people interested in
horses and equitation. Moreover, I feel it to be my duty toward
the sport of riding to write this book. Repeated sojourns in
foreign countries—in Germany, England, Switzerland, the
United States, and Canada—where I met riders of other con-
tinents and different backgrounds have contributed to this
decision, and, therefore, I want to dedicate this book to the
young and enthusiastic riders of this world.

I had my first contact with the horse when, in my earliest

days, I spent hours watching the soldiers of my father's regiment grooming their horses, exercising them, and following the severe pattern of military drill. With serious application I tried to imitate with my rocking horse what I had seen in the barracks school and longed impatiently for the day when I would sit on a real horse instead of on a wooden one. At the age of eight I was lifted by the groom on to one of my father's horses—without his knowledge, of course!—and led around in the courtyard of the barracks. I was thoroughly happy and so proud to sit on a big horse and not on a pony. I felt like a great rider!

When my father became aware of what was going on and realized my great enthusiasm, he ordered a serious and bearded sergeant from his regiment to give me lessons. First he was to teach me the correct seat on the longe. He was a grim man and so were his ways of teaching. He longed me without stirrups, as should be done, but the hard army saddle rubbed my skin off in places that became obvious when red patches appeared on my gray riding breeches. Still, my unlimited passion for riding made me suffer silently and unflinchingly. Only when, on the second day, the sergeant tried to make me clear a hurdle on the longe and I crashed to the ground each time was my confidence in myself and in my teacher completely shattered. I began to dread my riding lessons in which I found none of the "happiness of this world" on my poor horse's back. Nevertheless, even this harsh method of teaching proved fruitful: much later, when I had pupils of my own, I took care not to introduce them to the fundamentals of riding in the same manner. Even negative experiences in life may lead to a positive result: never let the enthusiasm of a young rider be undermined by harsh methods.

There was rich experience, positive and negative, to be gained during my military training in the cavalry, beginning with the first drill of the soldiers and continuing through three years at the Cavalry School. Later I enlarged my knowledge when I prepared my army horses for competition, which included Three-day Events as well as jumping and dressage classes. My success in these competitions apparently led my superiors to consider me eligible for a period of training at the Spanish Riding School. There I remained posted for two full years instead of the usual six months to a year.

At this time-honored institute I was privileged to have as my teachers the three famous head riders: Polak, Zrust, and Lindenbauer. They conveyed to me the most fundamental understanding, namely, that the classical art of riding as taught at the Spanish Riding School is based on the same foundation essential for every kind of riding: confidence between horse and rider; mutual understanding; and a thorough knowledge of the capabilities of the four-legged partner.

During several years spent as a riding instructor at the Cavalry School, where officers were trained to be riding teachers in the regiments, I had the opportunity to enhance my knowledge of schooling horses and riders. Also I realized the importance of a psychological approach to the pupils as well as to the horses, since the aim is to instruct both creatures, horses and riders, and make work enjoyable for both.

For twenty-six years I was Director of the Spanish Riding School, the oldest riding academy in the world, and was responsible for it during the Second World War and the immense difficulties afterward. By personal engagement as a rider and teacher, I had to maintain the standard of the School in spite of the completely altered and often very precarious circumstances. The proof that the standard was maintained at a very high level was furnished by the triumphant successes of the Spanish Riding School wherever it appeared—in the splendid riding hall in Vienna as well as on tours through Europe, the United States, and Canada.

Since retiring from the School, I have found ample opportunity to contribute to the development of dressage riding in England, Canada, and the U.S.A. by giving lectures and training courses and by demonstrating on horseback the rules of classical riding. Often I have been able to add to my own experience, for the rider goes on learning as long as he lives. Frequently there have been improperly trained horses that had to be corrected. While hitherto I had built my lessons on a progressive method, now it was important not only to see the faults right away but also to find the possibility of correction within the reach of the capabilities of the rider. I have learned a great deal in these past years without, however, deviating from the classical principles consolidated through the years. I have been confirmed in my belief that with riding lessons, psychological insight is equally as important as practical knowledge. This approach prohibits adopting a set pattern and forces the instructor to follow an individual method with each pupil, and the importance of this cannot be stressed too often.

Since my first trip to the United States in 1950, I have observed with interest the development of the sport of riding on this continent. Even long before this trip I had had the opportunity to see American officers at the Olympic Games in Berlin (1936), London, (1948), and Helsinki (1952), and to discuss their difficulties in adjusting to the standards of international riding. After the cavalry was disbanded in 1950, dressage was hardly known and much less practiced by civilian riders. I was the more astonished some ten years later when I found not only a widespread interest in this kind of riding but also saw performances I had not expected after my experiences in 1950, especially as there were practically no experienced trainers to be had. The Americans tried to cope with the situation by engaging experts from overseas, a solution that was unfortunately often exploited by Europeans. Many an "expert" advertised and offered himself to the highest bidders but did not possess the necessary knowledge and abilities. His good-natured pupils would listen full of confidence but, being unfamiliar with the basic requirements of this new kind of riding, would find him out too late when they were already lost in a maze of contradictions. Either the prospective dressage riders would resign or, when they were particularly dogged, would look for a "new man" from whom they hoped to obtain better results. On the whole, this is rather a sad chapter and not a flattering one for these false prophets of equitation.

Considering the fact that there are very few genuine riding instructors apart from those impostors I have just described, it is with appreciation that I have noted the development of dressage riding and the standard that has been reached. Credit is due to numerous dressage clubs which endeavor to raise the standard of their members by discussions, lectures, and practical demonstrations. I welcomed the opportunity of such meetings to give advice, hold conferences, and try to answer all sorts of equestrian problems. And I was pleased to note these riders' seriousness and dedication and absolute will to learn.

These observations have reminded me of my obligation to the sport of riding and have also shown me how to help enthusiastic young riders by theoretical explanations. As in every sport, so with riding, theory is proved by practical demonstration. But action should always be preceded by knowledge, and knowledge is provided by theory which shows the best line to take. Theory and practice cannot be separated.

So I will try to be as clear as possible in the hope that this book may give the reader knowledge and understanding for his riding lessons. If this aim is reached, I will be rewarded for my work, which I have, in any event, undertaken with enthusiasm.

1

THE TEACHER
AND THE PUPIL

1. What is expected from a riding instructor

From a riding teacher you should expect the same qualities required of every good teacher: he should have a thorough knowledge of the subject he is teaching and he should be capable of putting himself into the place of his pupil. In addition, with a riding teacher there should be an understanding of his assistant, the horse, whose behavior often decides success or failure.

The riding instructor will cope most easily with his task when he succeeds in thinking from his pupil's point of view and grasps his physical as well as psychological problems. Physical difficulties will be best understood by a teacher who remembers his own beginnings on horseback, that is, by one who is or was a rider himself. Psychological problems present greater difficulties, for they necessitate understanding the character and mind of the pupil. This ability is not given to everyone. Therefore it may happen that an excellent rider does not prove to be a good teacher, while another, though not able to demonstrate the art of classical riding to perfection, can convey the essence of it to his pupils.

It should be assumed, of course, that the teacher is capable of riding and has mastered the fundamentals of training. The ideal riding instructor will be one who at any given moment can demonstrate an exercise on horseback as correctly as he demands it from his pupil. It may happen, however, that he fails in his attempt, as, for instance, when the fault is too deeply rooted in the horse. Then he should prove to be above the situation and acknowledge his failure instead of trying to cover it up with hackneyed explanations or, worse, roughness to the horse. Needless to say, he must repeat his attempt until he succeeds, even if he spends more time on eradicating this fault. Such incidents may convey additional knowledge of what and how much to demand from pupil and horse.

Three traits of character are an absolute must with any successful riding teacher: he must have self-control, patience, and be free of any false ambition.

Self-control will enable him to accept calmly any progress, be it ever so small, as well as setbacks or even failure. He will not allow himself any thoughtless actions out of anger, knowing that he would set a bad example and relinquish his own right to demand self-control from his pupil. During the lesson he should not by the tone of his voice or by the expression of his face reveal that his pupil has disappointed him, for he should avoid discouraging him. Anything that might help to encourage the pupil, on the other hand, should by all means be mentioned. On no account should the riding instructor appear disinterested and apathetic during the lesson. It should be his constant endeavor, on the contrary, to find new ways and a different approach whenever difficulties arise.

It is part of the riding teacher's self-control to try to remain steady in his actions and his behavior and to suppress occasional bad moods to which all of us are subject. There is nothing more detrimental to a lesson than a teacher who corrects mistakes very calmly on one day and becomes vociferous on the next on the very same occasion. This will confuse the pupil and make him unable to recognize and himself feel his faults. Certainly constant manners are not easy, especially not in our hectic times, but it is worth trying to achieve them, as they help to consolidate the pupil's respect for his teacher.

Patience should be a virtue of the rider and also the highest principle of every successful riding teacher. He should endeavor to inspire his pupil with his patience, which will calm him and help him to overcome any difficulties much more easily while rash reactions would make him even more nervous. The instructor should continuously demonstrate this patience in dealing with horse and rider, encouraging the latter to follow his example. He should never expect patience from his pupil when he himself gives way to anger and impatience. This would mean preaching water and drinking wine.

The riding instructor should be free from any false ambition, which is much harder than it may seem at first mention, vanity being a driving power that may do much harm. Certainly every teacher should strive for progress with his pupils but not success at any cost, as, for instance, in order to impress spectators. With riding, progress is often less obvious to the non-initiated onlooker than to the expert, especially when the aim is to consolidate the foundation which is of such eminent importance for correct work. It is, therefore, an unforgivable mistake to show some tricks to the detriment of basic instruction—a mistake that the rider will pay for later.

The riding teacher is expected to know and to convey to his pupils that the measure of progress will not be the same with all students. A level will be reached in a few days by one rider, while another pupil will take a longer time. Students will also alternate in their achievements, one overtaking the other in the course of training and sometimes being overtaken in turn during another period of work. Consequently, the experienced riding teacher should never weigh the accomplishments of his pupils against each other and draw conclusions as to their progress. Considering the object of training as well as the road covered so far, he will size up the individual advance and ascertain that the correct direction has been maintained. It is an excellent psychological tactic to bring work to an end after a well-performed exercise. This gives the teacher the opportunity to compliment his pupil, thus encouraging him and making him look forward to the next riding lesson. The horse, too, will take it as a reward for a well-performed exercise when taken to the stables right afterward.

In conclusion, a riding instructor is expected to be sincerely attached to the horse and to understand the nature of this loyal partner. As a rider he should know how to develop the beauty of the horse's movements and how to convey this knowledge to his pupils. As a teacher he must be able to comprehend the mind of his students, especially when there is a great difference of age, and do his best to encourage his pupils to take pleasure in the sport of riding. At the same time, he should know that there is never an end to learning and be forever prepared to enlarge his own knowledge by new experiences. If he fulfills these requirements and also goes a straight way in his life, he will set an example for his pupils as a rider and as a gentleman.

2. What the riding instructor expects from his pupil

It should be every pupil's serious endeavor to learn as much as possible from his teacher and to enjoy the process of learning. With a rider this rule is even more applicable, for his aim is to learn not only to exercise his body in this new sport but also to guide his horse and control his moods and movements. Consequently, the riding teacher should expect his pupil to follow his orders without qualification and to be willing to work hard in order to reach the goal set. By his experience the conscientious instructor is to show his pupil the line to take and to cultivate and develop his abilities. The pupil's contribution to success is an honest affection for the horse, confidence in his teacher, and, again, much patience.

The rider should not regard his horse as a tool or an instrument of sport with which to satisfy his personal ambition, nor should he use him as a toy for his pastime. He should appreciate and love him as a living creature with a right to have a character of his own, with weak and strong points just like a human being. This attitude will make him understand his four-legged partner and will lay the foundation for confidence, which is the best guarantee for any success.

Confidence in his teacher, too, is expected from the pupil, and proof that he tries honestly to follow his instructor's directions and is not tempted to thwart them by ideas of his own not based on experience. To what degree the student is able to follow his teacher's orders depends largely on his physical abilities, but what counts is the visible effort and earnest will to obey.

There is one axiom that every prospective rider should never lose sight of: to become a rider takes patience and again endless patience. It is the only way to obtain progress and success, while the absence of this virtue will entail setbacks and failure. Actions committed out of impatience, though they may seem ever so insignificant, may in one second annihilate advance that has been obtained in weeks of hard work. This patience is nothing else but the visible result of self-control which is to be cultivated by riding and is of the greatest importance throughout the entire training from modest beginning up to the highest possible level. Every student should remember this and act accordingly.

Every sensible riding instructor knows that there is often a wide gap between good will and capability which has to be considered when teaching. When instructing on horseback, the teacher must limit his explanations to short comments and, in the interest of horse and rider, should expect that his directions be executed in silence. As the pupil has to concentrate on the lesson, he must follow or try to follow the commands of the teacher without comment, even if they do not seem clear to him at the moment. This does not mean, however, that the pupil should mechanically obey like a puppet. After dismounting he may and should ask his teacher questions about anything that is not clear to him and have it explained.

It seems necessary and appropriate to say a few words about the equipment of the rider. As on tennis courts, for instance, white is generally worn, so with riding there are certain rules as to the rider's appearance. He should wear breeches and boots or jodhpurs and a riding coat or a pullover. A serious rider should choose boots rather than jodhpurs, especially when training his own horse, for they allow him to apply the leg aids much more precisely. It is advisable to wear a hat or, preferably, a hunting cap which provides protection in case of a fall. This is especially important when jumping or riding cross-country. Gloves are not only prescribed by protocol but also help to prevent the reins from sliding from the rider's hand and protect the tender skin between the fingers. Girls should gather their hair in a net or pin it up in such a way that it does not fly about their heads. Spurs are worn when riding but not when walking in the street. A well-groomed appearance gives a certain style to riding and underlines the pleasure a person takes in this sport.

Of course, it is often impossible for a beginner to procure

the entire outfit at once and he will have to make shift in the meantime. But it should be expected from every riding student that he appears in clean and neat clothes, thus proving his respect for his riding teacher and the riding school. To be a rider means to behave in a chivalrous way, which should be apparent even in the smallest details.

3. The relationship between teacher and pupil

The relationship between pupil and teacher is of such decisive importance for the lessons that it is worth while discussing it in a separate chapter. There are a number of circumstances that should be remembered by both.

The aim being the same for both teacher and pupil, four basic elements are necessary for obtaining progress and success. First, teacher and pupil have to get to know each other; they will have to gain confidence in each other and find a mutual basis of sympathy and sincerity.

Before beginning the lessons the riding teacher should talk to his pupil, learn his background and, above all, his ideas about riding. He should know what his pupil expects from the lessons, whether it is true dedication or whether he is propelled by dreams of winning ribbons and showing off in public. It will help the instructor a great deal in his teaching if he knows the underlying motives. It is equally necessary to know the pupil's attitude toward the horse, which is of great importance for the entire process of teaching. Every rider is expected to look upon his horse as a friend with a character of his own and who, according to his intelligence, has a right to be treated as an individual. The rider should never think that his horse is stupid—which unfortunately happens quite often—and try to degrade him as his slave. Slaves will never appear as proud and beautiful as it is desired a horse should be. It is the pleasure a horse takes in his work that makes him appear beautiful and gives brilliance to his movements.

The student, too, should become acquainted with his teacher and respect and appreciate him. If he has some idea of the teacher's previous life and achievements, it will be easier for him to accept his authority, to follow his advice without qualification, and to take him as an example of conduct. The achievements of the instructor and his reputation as a teacher and a rider will make the pupil look up to him. A teacher who demonstrates that he never demands anything but what he can do himself will be halfway along the road to progress and success. He should, however, take care never to idealize himself or to exaggerate his successes. Reputation built on imaginary achievements will have a short life. The initial enthusiasm of the student would give way to even greater disenchantment.

To set an example of conduct implies a great obligation. It is only human that each of us has his strong and his weak sides, and they will be present in varying degrees. A conscientious teacher will try to have a clear knowledge of his own character and to balance the positive and negative sides in such a way that he is able to set an example for his pupils, to inspire confidence and assert his authority.

On the basis of confidence the pupil will submit to his teacher, who will guide him on his way to knowledge and proficiency. This task is not at all easy and can be realized only by a teacher whose conduct proves the correctness of his reputation and refutes any false statements that may be reported about him. In the same manner, the pupil should endeavor to make his actions coincide with *his* assertions.

From this starting point, mutual understanding will develop so that work may proceed in harmony and with pleasure that grows from lesson to lesson as the student asks advice from his teacher and observes it strictly. The teacher corrects faults the very moment they appear, thus preventing formation of bad habits, and skillfully blends praise and criticism. Criticizing constantly may very easily discourage the pupil; therefore, it is advisable to mention a good point first before correcting a fault. It goes without saying that the slightest progress should be mentioned to the pupil, giving him new impulse on his way to perfection.

In this collaboration, while retaining full authority, the teacher will share the joys and woes with his pupil and enjoy progress and success with him.

When there are setbacks—there always are—he will help his pupil with his advice and strengthen his confidence in himself. Of course he will give greater moral support to an easily disheartened and doubtful rider than to an over-confident one. A conscientious instructor will be only too glad if he can convey the experience he has gained to his pupil and, with awareness of the pupil's capacities, make learning easy and pleasant for him. The ability to help an enthusiastic young rider will be the greatest reward for a teacher.

4. What the instructor should know about his assistant, the horse

While for most kinds of sport a tool or instrument is required, with riding we have to deal with a living creature which, beyond the care that has to be given to an inanimate thing, also demands treatment with affection and as an individual. A riding horse treated in this way may develop into an assistant for the riding teacher and be of invaluable help to him. In former times the school horses at the Spanish Riding School and at the cavalry schools, the honest troopers of the cavalry, and the school horses at the civilian riding institutes introduced the young riders to the ABCs of horsemanship and, according to their varying degrees of training, assisted the riding instructor in his task. The more advanced they were in their training, the greater was their help to him.

Nowadays when there is such a marked lack of riding instructors and an even greater one of suitable school horses, we think with nostalgia of those bygone times. The lack of school horses is, in fact, one of the greatest problems for teacher and pupil today. In the beginning the pupil has to try to adjust to the horse's movements and from his individual behavior draw conclusions as to his character and temperament. From this point he may become his horse's friend. The instructor, too, should know the school horse, understand his movements and his temperament. He must be able to judge his characteristics and then give his pupil the correct advice. In most cases the teacher will have to prepare the horse for his pupil, riding him before the actual lesson. This is even more important if the instructor uses several horses for his lessons and the student does not ride the same horse every time. However, in the interest of the student, changing horses frequently should be avoided as much as possible.

It also happens that pupils bring their own horses for the lessons, and they are often untrained ones. In this case the instructor has to teach both horse and rider at the same time. Again he himself will have to ride the horse at regular intervals. Pluvinel, writing in 1623, maintained that an efficient riding instructor should be capable of teaching both rider and untrained horse at the same time, but, of course, such a horse will only gradually, as he progresses in his own training, grow to be the instructor's assistant.

I have stressed the relationship between pupil and teacher and between both and the horse for a good reason: in our world of rapid technical development and of thinking in terms of the masses, the value of the individual is easily forgotten.

2

BASIC THEORY OF RIDING

For any kind of work, the subject should be thoroughly understood; any craftsman and artist must have a theoretical knowledge of his sphere just as the rider should understand the basic rules of riding and the role of the animal, for it is not sufficient to know only that a horse has four legs. This theoretical preparation should precede the actual riding lessons because there is not time for it once in the school ring. In this book the subject will be mentioned only briefly for the same reason. The theory of training, the definition of the paces, and the principles of equitation, as well as the detailed explanations of the aids for the various exercises and the progressive method of schooling have been covered in my previous book, *The Complete Training of Horse and Rider*. The present guide discusses the situation from the standpoint of the teacher and will give merely a digest of the essential theory.

It is the aim of a rider to be able to move in balance on his horse's back and perform various exercises with him. This sport should yield pleasure not only for the rider but also for the horse, who should be calm, supple, and obedient, comfortable in his movements, and should submit to his rider without constraint. All exercises that promote the physical training of the horse will help to reach this aim. The degree of physical training a horse has reached may in turn be determined by means of these exercises.

The horse moves in three paces: walk, trot, and canter. At the walk we hear four hoofbeats. At the trot there are two hoofbeats to be heard when the diagonal legs touch the ground (for instance, right foreleg and left hind leg, which is the right diagonal). Between the two hoofbeats there is a moment of suspension when for an instant none of the four legs touches the ground. This moment of suspension makes the trot more difficult for the rider to sit through than the walk. The canter consists of a series of bounds. We hear three hoofbeats, which are followed by a moment of suspension; for instance, 1. right hind leg, 2. left hind leg and

The walk

right forefoot together, 3. left forefoot, suspension. We speak of a canter left when the left forefoot is the last to touch the ground and of a canter right in the opposite case.

It is important that the horse move his legs rhythmically, which proves that he is balanced physically as well as mentally, thus allowing the rider to sit correctly and have a good feeling. In all three paces there may be different speeds according to how much ground the horse gains to the front: the normal speed which is chosen by the horse when he moves on his own at liberty, the extended pace, and the collected pace. It is easier for the rider to maintain a correct seat, which does not disturb the balance and the movements of the horse, at the collected and normal speeds than at the extended one.

We speak of a halt when the horse comes to a standstill. In this exercise he should carry his weight evenly distributed on all four legs, should stand quietly in the direction

The trot

of the movement (and not be crooked), and should concentrate on his rider.

Contact is the connection of the rider's hand with the mouth of the horse through the reins and the bit. It is the means by which to guide and to collect the horse. The rider should never try to force the contact by pulling at the reins, which would restrict the horse's urge to go forward. On the contrary, it is the horse that should seek contact with the hand of the rider without lying on the bit and pulling.

The immediate and visible result of contact is the position of the head. Together with the carriage of the neck, the position of the head is of great importance for the horse's balance. In the initial stage of training it should be free, that is, the horse should stretch his head and neck forward more and carry them lower than in the collected paces and in an advanced period of training. In the latter cases the line of the face should be nearly vertical while the neck is arched and the

The canter

head brought nearer to the chest. However, the face line must never come behind the vertical, which would hinder the horse from going forward. Nor should the head come up, because then the horse would drop his back and in this uncomfortable position would lose his balance. Besides, the rider cannot sit correctly on a hollow back.

When moving on straight lines, head and neck should be straight. In turns and circles, the horse should be bent evenly from head to tail according to the arc of the circle or turn.

Collection is an increased action of the hind legs, which are made to step well under the body in the direction of the hoofprints of the forelegs; the horse becomes shorter in his body with his back arched correctly; head and neck are carried higher while the line of the face becomes nearly vertical. Therefore, to collect the horse does not mean to screw his head down by pulling at the reins with hard hands as may often be seen. It means to increase the pushing aids of the legs and drive the horse toward the reins which remain applied. Correct collection may be obtained by degrees according to the progress in training and through gradually working in the collected paces. It intensifies the horse's suppleness and increases the flexibility of the hind legs, which are made to carry a greater portion of the horse's weight as well as that of the rider. By thus relieving the forehand it helps to prevent wearing out the horse's legs prematurely.

An important section of the basic rules of riding is the knowledge of the aids which represent the language between horse and rider. It was profound thought that through the ages has given the name "aids" to the communication from rider to horse, for the rider should help his horse to understand him. This means that the horse must never be afraid of the aids and that the rider should always apply them in the same manner and with the same intensity and have sufficient patience until his horse has understood.

The aids are directed to the horse's hearing and to his responsiveness to touch. The hearing is extremely well developed and much more sensitive to the various sounds and modulations than is generally assumed. The click of the tongue arouses his attention and will make the horse go forward in the same way as does the crack of the longe whip or the sound of the whip lash dropped to the ground. A commanding tone of voice will also send him forward, while he will be calmed by a soft-spoken word and accept it as a reward.

The majority of the aids are addressed to the horse's responsiveness to touch. In fact, with the fully trained dressage horse these aids alone transmit the rider's commands. Therefore, the rider must preserve the sensitiveness of the horse's mouth and make use of the reactions of the horse's body to the rider's legs and the distribution of his weight. The ultimate aim toward which the rider works—and which is demanded at the Olympic Games—is to guide the horse with invisible and inaudible aids. The onlooker should have the impression that two creatures are fused together, one thinking and the other executing the thoughts.

According to their effect we distinguish pushing aids (leg and weight aids, click of the tongue, riding whip, longe whip, and spurs) and restraining aids (rein aids and weight aids).

It is important to know that the degree of the aids should vary according to the temperament and the sensitiveness of the horse as well as to the standard of training he has reached. Moreover, the rider should never forget that an increased measure of the same aid may be understood by the horse as a punishment. For thousands of years the maxim has been maintained that "The art of riding is based on the judicious administration of reward and punishment." Today we note with regret that, *vis-à-vis* the age-old principle, the administration of punishment has been observed much more than that of reward. In our time many people advocate the abolishment of capital and other severe punishments for man. Should riders not follow this example and use milder methods on our horses who are helpless and at our mercy? Our four-legged comrades will return this kindness with unfaltering loyalty. And if we remember to reward them at any appropriate moment, then not only will we riders experience the happiness of this world but our horses, too, will be happy creatures.

3

SYSTEMATIC
RIDING INSTRUCTION

5. The first goal

As in life, so with riding, we must fix our eyes on a goal and advance toward it in a straight direction. To be able to follow this principle we should not make too difficult demands in the beginning but choose an aim within reach of abilities. This will prevent us from losing sight of the goal and advancing in a wrong direction. Having reached the first goal, we may concentrate on the next higher one, thus progressing step by step toward the top. This is true for the pupil as well as for the teacher. Although the need for methodical planning of instruction appears to be so evident, it is rarely observed to the letter. Therefore, it seems necessary to explain it here in detail.

How often it may be observed that a rider who is just able to sit on his horse already has dreams about going to horse shows and winning ribbons. But there are also teachers who, with the smallest progress of their pupil, see in him the future Olympic candidate. It sounds absurd but I have witnessed it myself. Such exaggeration is not to be regarded purely as bad judgment, for it may also have a bad effect from the pedagogical point of view: unsound ambition or heightened complacency might be unduly nourished.

The first aim of the instructor is to lay the foundation of the right attitude of his pupil toward the horse. He will introduce him to grooming and care, to saddling and bridling and will build up his confidence. The next step is to teach him the correct seat and cultivate his feeling for the rhythm of the horse's movements. The duration of time necessary for this first step will vary with each pupil and depend on his talent and the experience he has had so far. It makes a difference whether this is his first contact with the horse or whether he has had previous experience. If he has had regular riding lessons on classical principles, the teacher does not spend much time on fundamental details but may continue where his predecessor has left off. If, however, the pupil has deviated from the right path it is generally more time-consuming than with a beginner, because it is more difficult to eliminate faults which have become established.

At any rate, even with a rider with some experience, the teacher should go rapidly through the preliminaries in order to ascertain the correctness of the previous instruction. The teacher should be prepared to encounter difficulties with a certain category of students who frequently change their teachers and consequently are usually lost in a maze of contradictions. These pupils also reveal a trait of character detrimental to the making of a good rider: inconsistency.

We have discussed the pupil's attitude toward the horse on page 9 in "What the riding instructor expects from his pupil," and it will be mentioned again throughout the book. The teacher will observe his pupil attentively and never tolerate outbursts of temperament or bad moods. He must nip fits of anger in the bud.

The relationship with the horse is easily established with students who take care of their horses themselves, as is often the case nowadays. As the horse is confined to the stables for twenty-two hours or more every day, he should be as comfortable as possible. Not many horse owners, especially in the cities, can put their horses in a paddock where they can move freely for several hours a day. Often there are tie stalls only, in which the horses have just enough room to lie down and cannot roll. These horses stand with their heads to the wall and to take the weight off their feet have to move from one leg to the other. Besides the riding lessons, these horses should be walked frequently and care must be taken that the chain in the stall is not so short that the horse cannot lie down. On the other hand, it should not be so long that the horse may step into the chain and injure himself. It is most advantageous to have chains that run through a ring next to the manger and that have a weight of lead or wood at the end, thus establishing a light contact with the halter. The throat latch of the halter should not be too tight and interfere with the horse's breathing.

A horse will be much happier in a box stall, and every rider who loves his horse should endeavor to put him up in one. It must be large enough for the horse to move about comfortably and roll without hurting himself.

In both cases care must be taken that the stall is clean. The horse needs good bedding, preferably straw. If, however, he eats too much of it, sawdust or shavings may be used. It should not be forgotten to clean the manger before feeding: leftovers from previous feedings may turn sour and spoil the fresh oats. Regular feeding is important for the horse's health. There should be three meals a day, and the horse should be fed at least two hours before working. If a horse is worked in the morning it is advisable to distribute the ration of oats as follows: one fourth in the morning; one to two fourths at noon; and the remainder at night, preferably toward six o'clock. Hay should be given in the same measure and the horse should have enough of it. Before being fed oats he should be given hay and water. This prevents him from eating his oats too greedily. Another way to curb this greed is to mix the oats with chaff (finely chopped straw). Always and especially in warm weather the horse should be given sufficient water, which should not be too cold, particularly in winter. If the horse returns to the stables hot from work, he should not drink until having cooled down completely, which sometimes may be as long as two hours.

To give neither feed nor water before work or a horse show is an unpardonable method to calm down a high-spirited horse and cool his temperament. And yet it is more often employed than we care to think. No athlete would be expected to give top performances on an empty stomach. How can we demand such things from a mute creature entrusted to our care?

As a person washes and tidies before beginning his day's work, the horse should be groomed every day and before and after work, but never during feeding time. Even the animal should be left in peace while eating. For grooming, the horse should be tied with a halter and a rope to two rings in the wall. Here he is under control and does not adopt any bad habits such as turning about in his box, or kicking or nipping his groom. The coat is rubbed with straw, and dust is brushed off with a brush. A wet sponge cleans eyes, lips, nostrils, and under the tail. A curved piece of iron, the hoof pick, removes sand, dirt, or manure from the sole of the foot. The hoofs are washed with water and a brush. The horny part of the foot is treated with hoof oil, which, however, should not be applied in a thick layer because with dust and sand it would form a crust. It should be rubbed into the hoof as we do when we massage cream into our hands after washing. Warm hoofs must never be washed with cold water immediately after strenuous work, for this might entail serious damage.

These procedures should be rounded out through practical experience which is most easily acquired by a rider who takes care of his horse himself. Also, he has the advantage of rapidly establishing contact with his horse and gaining his confidence. But those riders whose horses are brought saddled and bridled into the riding school should be interested in what goes on before the horse is ready. They should consult the teacher and not hesitate to watch carefully an old and skilled groom at work. With some knowledge of stable work, the rider will be able to control the correctness of his horse's care and, if necessary, direct an unskilled or untrained groom, such as we encounter very often these days.

Thus care and grooming are explained in a nutshell. In the same brief way, a few things which should be known by every riding pupil are to be said about saddles and bridles. Saddling the horse demands special knowledge and care. The correct position of the saddle is decisive for the horse's movement as well as for the correct seat of the rider, which in turn is important for the balance of the horse. The saddle should be placed on the center of the horse's back in such a way that the girths will lie on the true ribs. It is with intention that I have said "placed" and not thrown on the horse's back as may be seen so often. Apart from the fact that the saddle will get into disorder, there is the chance that the horse, being easily frightened by nature, will be startled. Proceeding slowly and carefully while speaking softly to the horse will, however, consolidate his confidence.

It is of advantage to begin to saddle right after grooming, thus gaining sufficient time before work to tighten the girths slowly and gradually. If the girths are tightened too quickly, the horse may feel uneasy, blow himself up, and even get up on his hind legs and fall over backwards. The best way to prevent this is to fasten the girths lightly to begin with and tighten them hole by hole, waiting in between while making other preparations such as bridling and bandaging. The horse should be tied by the halter, for he should not lie down and roll, which would damage the saddle.

It is of importance for the rider that the lowest point of the saddle should lie just in front of the central point. If the saddle is low behind, the rider's seat will glide backwards and the upper part of his body will also lean back. Then his legs and knees come too far forward and cannot influence the horse correctly. Besides, the whole saddle would slide forward and the rider's weight would shift onto the forehand of the horse. Most horses are saddled too far forward or, by the movement of the horse, the saddle creeps forward. In this case the horse must be resaddled, that is, the rider dismounts, loosens the girths, and replaces the saddle in the correct position, gliding it from the front backwards, smoothing the hair, and retightening the girths. On the other hand, the saddle should not be placed too far back on the horse so that the girths lie on the false ribs, which would cause similar difficulties and have the same effect as when the girths were tightened too rapidly.

When tightening the girths a fault is frequently committed which entails bad habits that are difficult to eliminate later. During this procedure the horse must be prevented from turning about or creeping back, from pushing his groom with his head or trying to nip at him. On principle, therefore, the horse should be tied with a halter when being saddled. If he is already bridled, the rider proceeds as follows. As a rule the girths are tightened from the left side. The rider passes his left arm through the reins which lie over the horse's neck.

Now he has the horse's movements under control. The left arm with the reins prevents the horse from evading toward the right side. If he tries to turn to the left side, which is rare, the rider leans his arm against the horse's neck.

When choosing or fitting the saddle, care must be taken that with the girths tightened there is a two-finger space between the withers of the horse and the saddle. If this rule is not observed and the saddle touches the withers, it may cause saddle sores, which take a long time to heal.

The preparations are completed by replacing the halter with the bridle just before leading the horse into the schooling. For training, the rider uses two bridles: the snaffle and the double bridle. For schooling young horses and young riders, the snaffle bit should always be used, while the double bridle is reserved for horse and rider more advanced in training. But even with the fully trained riding horse it is of advantage if the snaffle is substituted for the double bridle now and again. This method preserves the sensitiveness of the horse's mouth.

The reins are placed over the horse's neck and the halter is removed. The right hand is passed under the horse's jaws and the thumb holds the center of the bridle in front of the horse's face and above his head so that the bit is in front of the horse's mouth. Speaking softly will prevent the horse from getting frightened and causing difficulties, especially for the first few times. In most cases the horse opens his mouth when the bit touches his front teeth and allows the bit to be placed in his mouth. If he clenches his teeth, which may happen sometimes also with older horses, the rider presses his left forefinger on the toothless bars on the lower jaw, which will make the horse open his mouth and accept the bit. It would take too much space here to discuss the necessary width and breadth of the bit. Let us just say that the thicker the bit the milder its effect on the horse's mouth, which is especially important with the unskilled hand of a beginner. The bit should not be placed too high in the horse's mouth and pull up the corners of the lips. Nor should it lie too low and touch the teeth. The noseband should be fastened tightly but must not lie too low on the horse's nose and hinder breathing. Also, the horse must be able to accept titbits from the rider's hand. The throat latch, however, should be fitted so loosely that the width of a hand may be passed between it and the horse's jawbone.

When leading the horse, the rider walks at his left side. The reins are passed to the front over the horse's head (with the double bridle, the snaffle reins only are used to lead) and the loop is placed over the right thumb. Passing the forefinger of the same hand between both reins, the rider holds them tightly right under the horse's chin. Then he has his horse under control at any time without pulling at his mouth. It is better to lead the horse in this manner than with the reins lying on the horse's neck the way they were placed during bridling. In case of shying the horse may not tear himself loose as easily when the pupil holds the end of the reins in his hand. On no account should the horse be led by one rein only.

Up to the moment of mounting, the stirrups should be secured by running the iron up to the stirrup bar on the leather next to the saddle and tucking the leather down through the iron so that it does not dangle. After dismounting, both stirrups are secured in the same way.

So much about the preparation of the horse for work. These are fundamental rules which should be supplemented by practical demonstrations and by consulting books on horse care and training.

Saddling and bridling when carried out by the pupil and controlled and corrected by the teacher represent a most effective introduction to the riding lesson. The foundation of confidence between horse and rider is laid, and to create that confidence should be a constant endeavor, like an unbroken thread, through the entire process of riding and training. The horse becomes acquainted with the rider's voice and movements and will not face a completely strange creature when the lesson begins. The rider, in turn, will learn that the horse is by no means a "wild beast" or a stupid animal as sometimes described by thoughtless persons. He will find out that most horses are easily frightened and then have a tendency to flee. They will rarely attack a person, but when there is no possibility of flight, they might make use of their means of defense, which is biting, rearing, or kicking with their hind legs. The more intelligence an animal possesses the more effectively he will defend himself when he feels intimidated or mistreated. It is deliberately that I use the word "defend," for experience has taught me that there is no such thing as a horse born vicious. A horse is not vicious by nature but is made so by bad and rude treatment. It is often maintained that horses of certain breeds have a tendency to viciousness. They may be very sensitive and difficult to handle because of being hot-blooded and high-strung and will react more violently to wrong treatment. If such a horse has a bad reputation, the trainer might approach him more cautiously and subconsciously adopt an apprehensive attitude, thus irritating the horse and inducing him to some reaction. In most cases, violent insubordination of a horse is caused by the fear of man or by the fact that he does not understand what is required of him or is unable to carry out a demanded exercise. The rider should seek the fault in himself before blaming the horse.

When observing the horse carefully the pupil will win his horse's confidence and in turn gain confidence in him and also realize that horses usually cling to their habits. This will be the first step toward a mutual understanding which is vital for the performance of a horse and even more so for the progress of the rider. The thorough knowledge of the horse teaches us to draw conclusions about his behavior from the most insignificant signs and movements. This is why the instructor must study his four-legged assistant and draw the attention of his pupil to these signs and warn him in time—especially during the very first lessons. When a horse shies away from an object or from a certain spot or a noise—the hearing and sight of the horse are especially well developed—he will generally signal it first by raising his head and pricking his ears, also by a reluctance to advance and by edging away from the object of his fear before taking to flight. As horses have a very good memory, these incidents will usually occur on the same spot or be caused by the same noises, so the teacher can avoid major mishaps by coming to his pupil's aid in time.

By a short order such as "Apply the reins!" or "Push him forward!" he may prevent the horse from running away, thus saving the young and helpless rider from a fall. Also, he should try to increase the horse's confidence by leading him up to the object of his fear and showing him the "stumbling block" while talking to him and caressing him. Doing so once will probably not suffice, and the procedure has to be repeated calmly again until confidence is established in both horse and rider. This is the only way to succeed, whereas shouting or using the whip would result in even greater fear on the part of the horse and complete helplessness of the rider. This is one more occasion for the teacher to demonstrate his patience and discipline.

The keen memory of the horse is, in fact, to be taken into account during the entire training. It helps the horse to understand the demands of his rider and is of great benefit in obtaining progress. The same faculty, however, may represent a serious impediment to training. It may happen that a horse remembers even after months that he had been frightened when passing a certain spot or had been severely punished and becomes nervous every time he nears this place. When a thoughtless rider frequently practices some exercises in a certain order, the horse will try in a very short time to anticipate the rider's aids. The conclusions the rider should draw from these situations are: moderation when administering punishment; patience when making the horse familiar with a dreaded object; and variation in the daily work in order to keep the horse's attention alert. Besides his excellent memory, the horse has a very good sense of direction which enables him to find his way back to the stables without fail even if he is miles away from it.

Just like any other creature, a healthy and well-kept horse is entitled to gaiety and playfulness which he will also announce by raising his head and pricking his ears and, according to his habit, express by bucking with a low head and high hind quarters, capriole-like leaps, or sudden turns. It will be easier for teacher and pupil to counter such outbursts with a horse that both know already than with an unfamiliar animal. This underlines once more the first goal in training: to get to know one's horse and to gain his confidence.

Having made his pupil familiar with the horse, the teacher then proceeds to the first and fundamental object of instruction: to teach the independent seat which enables the rider to sit without disturbing the horse's balance necessary for correct motion. We may speak of an independent seat when the rider makes use of the reins exclusively to guide his horse and never to maintain or regain his own lost balance. The knees must lie flat on the saddle and never move away from it, thus giving the seat the necessary firmness and allowing the lower legs to apply the pushing aids. The lower legs should not be used to take a firm grip on the horse's belly. The correct seat is relaxed and unconstrained and does not force the rider into an unnatural and stiff position. The ultimate object of riding must never be lost sight of: to give the rider a comfortable feeling on his horse in all situations, be it executing dressage figures in a ring, riding cross-country, or clearing the obstacles of a jumping course. He should sit upright and yet relaxed, and it is these apparently divergent factors that combine to make riding into an art.

The cultivation of the rider's feeling should also be kept in mind from the beginning, although it can be developed only gradually in the course of instruction. He must learn to feel when his horse moves correctly in balance and rhythm, going well forward, or if he advances incorrectly, thus hindering any progress. It will take a longer time to obtain the correct feeling than to learn the independent seat by constant correction of any faults or bad habits.

The time necessary to teach the correct seat will vary with different riders and depend on their age, physical proficiency, talent, any previous riding instruction, and, last but not least, on the horse. A young and agile person will certainly obtain the physical skill sooner and more easily than an older one, which does not mean, however, that a person advanced in age might not learn how to ride. On the contrary, serious determination and increased ability to concentrate—maybe even a little ambition—may outweigh physical shortcomings. It goes without saying that persons active in some other sport will have an advantage in their riding lessons over those who do not practice any sport at all. For the latter it is advisable to practice gymnastic exercises as a preparation to their riding lessons and as a compensation for the unaccustomed strain on their muscles.

Talent for riding, besides affection for the horse, is of

immeasurable value for successful training if recognized and correctly developed by the teacher. Here a gift is bestowed upon the student which, like well-invested capital, will continue to bring interest.

It is of crucial importance for both teacher and pupil what kind of horse may be used as the assistant in instruction. The perfect solution would be a fully trained riding horse, a school horse, that the teacher himself rides at regular intervals in order to be able to give appropriate advice to his pupil or to prove that failure was due to the pupil's ineptitude. By riding the horse regularly he will also eliminate faults caused by the young and unskilled rider.

But in most cases nowadays, old and somewhat lethargic riding horses are used as the teacher's assistant. Such horses have been through the ups and downs of life, have been blunted and more or less spoiled by clumsy hands. Very often it happens that the teacher is faced with the problem of a novice rider on a green horse whose training will demand a considerable stretch of time and frequent active interference on the part of the teacher. Nevertheless, it may have its advantages and be much easier than correcting an older and spoiled horse.

The different kinds of horses show us clearly the necessity of the varying length of training and also of the individual approach to teaching. The instructor must have a well-planned program but not succumb to a set pattern of work if he intends to bring his pupil along. It has been the object of the detailed discussion in this chapter to help to avoid unsuccessful methods or a complete lack of any method. It has been with a purpose also that the psychological side of the problem has been stressed, for today it is so often forgotten. Whenever difficulties occur in the course of training, it might be helpful to consult this chapter.

6. Training on the longe

A. ON A LONGE HORSE

Before beginning, teacher and pupil should seek an opportunity to discuss all details explained so far, thus reserving the riding lesson for practical instruction. The first contact, the first impression are influential for the co-operation of teacher and pupil. It may inspire enthusiasm in the young rider and make work easy and cheerful. By rudeness or carelessness, on the other hand, it might discourage him and even take away his pleasure in riding.

If the pupil has never been on horseback before, instruction should by all means begin on the longe. Work on the longe is the best guarantee of obtaining the independent seat. Besides, on the longe the teacher has the horse under his control and should try to avoid having the pupil be discouraged by falling from the horse right in the beginning.

Even with pupils who have had previous riding experience, it is preferable to begin instruction by a few lessons on the longe which offer the teacher the opportunity to observe his pupil's abilities. The duration of work on the longe varies according to the purpose in riding. A beginner whose wish it is to ride out and enjoy nature on his horse's back is generally given a shorter period on the longe until he has gained sufficient balance and is able to use the reins mainly for the guidance of his horse. Corrections of the seat, if necessary, may then be continued during the lessons in groups. Students who aim higher and intend to participate in competitions should have a much more thorough training on the longe. Lessons on the longe are never a waste of time, even for an advanced rider if he seeks the possibility of constantly correcting and improving his seat.

The current scarcity of efficient riding teachers has made a rare thing of longeing lessons in which the instructor deals with one pupil at a time. For it is preposterous and of no value whatsoever to try to longe two or three pupils at the same time on horses that run one behind the other while the teacher holds two or three longes in his hand. Therefore, correcting the seat while instructing riders in a group has become of greater importance even if it does not offer the advantages of proper longeing lessons. (Pages 51–56.)

Before entering the ring the rider, leading his horse in the correct manner described in the previous chapter, will have to make sure that he does not disturb other riders already at work. This is particularly important in a covered arena where he cannot see well from the outside. In most riding schools it is the custom to ask "Entrance clear?" which expression is also used before leaving the hall. Protocol of a well-run riding establishment and courtesy toward the other riders demand that the pupil bring his horse to a standstill on the center line parallel to the short side of the school where he will not risk disturbing anybody. If he has not seen his teacher before, it is obvious good manners to salute him, as is the practice in the riding schools of most countries.

For longeing, the horse is brought into the arena in a snaffle with a cavesson and side reins, and the saddle with the stirrups drawn up. Together with the instructor the student controls saddle and bridle if he has not saddled the horse himself under supervision of his teacher. Saddle and bridle should be correctly adjusted as described on pages 27–29. The cavesson should be fitted in such a way that the noseband lies below the cheekbones and on the nosebone and does not touch the gristle of the nose. Cheek strap and chin strap should be sufficiently tight to prevent the cavesson from chafing. The student pulls down the stirrups and under the supervision of the teacher adjusts the length of the leather by placing his fingertips on the stirrup bars with his arm outstretched and lengthening or shortening the leather until the stirrup touches his armpit. Further adjustments, if necessary, may be made after mounting. At the moment of saddling, the side reins were passed through the girth with one end while the other was secured and not left dangling. Now the side reins are fastened to the rings in the snaffle and the length adjusted until the horse adopts the correct position of his head and takes a light contact on the bit. It is advisable to leave the side reins at a comfortable length. Also they must be of the same length on both sides.

For mounting, the rider stands as close as possible on the left side of the horse, facing him. He takes the left rein with his left hand, gliding it slowly up to the withers. The right hand grasps the right rein which lies on the withers and places it in the left hand. Both reins are lightly applied and should maintain a light contact with the horse's mouth to make him stand quietly. The teacher, too, takes care of that by standing close to the horse's head and holding him by the longe, which is fastened to the center ring of the cavesson. The student grasps the left stirrup with his right hand and inserts his left foot so that the tread is up against his heel. The left knee is pressed firmly against the saddle without touching the horse's body with the tip of the boot, which would make the horse fidget. The left hand of the rider now grasps a few hairs of the mane just above the withers and the right hand grasps the cantle of the saddle. The rider pushes himself up with the right foot and, leaning slightly forward, lifts himself up until the right foot is level with the left. The right hand is now placed on the right flap on the saddle, the right leg with a bent knee swings high over the cantle, and the rider lowers himself gently into the saddle. On no account must he dump his whole weight on the horse's back as is so often done. He then turns his right foot inward and inserts it into the stirrup without looking down. While being mounted, the horse must stand still on all four legs until asked to move. In this case the teacher attends to that.

At a standstill the instructor will now explain the correct seat to his pupil. He makes the rider push his seat forward in the saddle until he sits correctly in its center. The seat should be well open to allow the rider to sit as deep as possible. A deep seat is a firm seat and will help him to maintain his balance in all situations. Both hips should be vertical to the saddle and should not be collapsed to one side. The rider's back rises straight from the hips, and the small of his back is braced without making a hollow spine. In spite of the upright position, the rider's back must always be supple and flexible, which allows him to follow smoothly all movements of the horse. The shoulders should be straight and the chest slightly arched without tenseness, and the shoulder blades lie flat against the back. A vertical line drawn through the rider's shoulders would form a right angle with the horse's spine.

The head is to be carried with a firm but not stiff neck, and the chin should be slightly drawn back. The rider's eyes should look straight forward over the ears of his horse and in the direction he rides. Looking down would make him bend his head forward and round his back, sitting with hunched shoulders.

The inside of the thighs should lie firmly along the saddle but not be pressed against it, which would make them tense. The thighs should form a slight angle with the hips, making the knee lie forward on the flap of the saddle. No gap should appear between the knee and the saddle, which would make the seat lose its firmness. The lower legs form a wide angle with the thigh and lie along the horse's body, hanging down by their own weight without tenseness. The calves must not be pressed against the horse's sides and act as a clutch. In this case the knees would open and lose their grip. The rider's foot is approximately at the height of the girth, with the toes turned inward and the heel the lowest point. This braces the muscles of the calves and so allows the rider to use the pushing aids of his legs correctly.

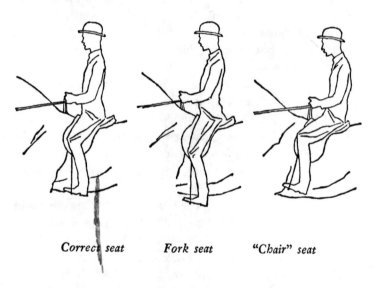

Correct seat   *Fork seat*   *"Chair" seat*

Then the teacher orders the pupil to take up the reins, one in each hand, flat between the little finger and the ring finger. The hand is formed into a fist. The ends of the reins come out over the index finger and are held down by the thumb. The loop of the ends of the reins should hang down freely between the right side of the horse's neck and the right rein.

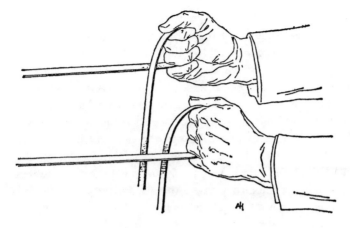

Correct way of holding reins of the snaffle

Having thus shaped the rider's seat as a sculptor would carve a statue, the instructor may set the horse in motion at a walk, provided that the pupil has understood the correct seat at a standstill. It requires considerable practice and an increased skill to be able to maintain this seat in the other paces. These first lessons on the longe will convey to the teacher a good idea of the temperament and character of his pupil.

The teacher makes the horse move on at a walk and takes him on a straight line from the center to the circumference of the circle where he will be longed. He will take care that the pupil does not hold on to the reins but leaves them sufficiently long to allow the horse a good stride. When moving off he should explain to the pupil that he must balance the upper part of his body in co-ordination with the horse's movements and not fall back when the horse moves off. In case of difficulties in this first lesson, if the horse does not move off or wants to remain straight instead of going on the circle, the teacher leads him on with the longe but must on no account try to push him forward with the whip. It might be necessary to lead him on the circle for several rounds and then move slowly back to the center while the pupil rides on the circle at a quiet walk. As a rule, work on the longe is begun on the left rein, on which side it is easier for the horse to get accustomed to going on a circle. The left rein is more familiar to the horse as he is usually led, saddled, mounted, etc., from the left.

When the horse moves calmly the pupil shortens the reins by making a knot to prevent them from dangling and lays them over the horse's neck. From this point on the instructor is directing the horse, controlling him with longe, side reins, and whip. The pupil is no longer responsible for guiding the horse and concentrates entirely on practicing his own balance and the position of his body in all movements and at the various paces of the horse. In this way he will most easily and quickly learn the independent seat necessary for any kind of riding. This result will be obtained even faster and better if after a few days of having become familiar with this new activity the pupil no longer uses the stirrups but removes them altogether from the saddle. Thus he learns to follow all movements and become one with his horse. Of course, this oneness will come gradually by slowly increasing the demands. Again it will depend on the talent of the rider, his temperament and discipline, as well as his determination to succeed.

The ambition of the pupil on one side and the intelligence and sympathetic understanding of the teacher on the other are the foundation of successful co-operation which will not fail to bear fruit. In this period of training it is the pupil's endeavor to maintain the seat his teacher has taught and explained at a halt. The instructor must bear in mind that it is difficult for the pupil in the beginning to maintain at a trot what he has been taught at a halt and a walk. It demands much patience on the part of the teacher to correct faults that occur over and over again. Correction must be administered logically. The instructor should not make the mistake of trying to correct everything at the same time. This would confuse and discourage the young rider. Therefore, the exercise should be calmly repeated, whereas shouting at the pupil would only make him even more nervous.

The horse's movements play an important part, according to whether they are stiff or supple. A well-trained horse would be the best assistant to the teacher—but is rarely to be had nowadays. Therefore, with horses with stiff movements the teacher, in order to maintain a smooth rhythm, should not demand too energetic a trot. When it is difficult for the rider to sit through the trot he may hold on to the saddle and pull his seat into it. Should the horse shy or make a sudden movement, the pupil is better prepared in this position. He can take h' upper part back instead of hunching his body forward, which would make him lose his seat. It is much better to hold on and sit correctly than to try to remain in the saddle by twisting the body or clutching the horse with one's calves.

As the horse moves on a circle on the longe, the pupil, besides learning about the movements, is introduced to riding turns. He learns to sit more on the inside seat bone and bring his outside shoulder sufficiently forward to make the shoulders form a right angle with the horse's spine. This imaginary line drawn through the shoulders of the rider would continue to the trainer in the center of the circle. As the pupil, according to the movements of the horse, generally slides to the outside, dropping his outside shoulder, he should hold on to the cantle of the saddle with his inside hand and to the pommel with his outside one.

The longe horse should go alternately on the left rein

and on the right one in order to form the rider's seat equally on both sides and to make him familiar with riding to different sides. For the horse, too, it is important to change reins as greater effort is demanded from the inside legs than from the outside ones when on a circle. For the change of rein the horse is taken into a walk first and then brought into the center of the circle by shortening the longe and calling "Come here." He is made to stand still by short actions of the longe if necessary. The teacher then rewards the horse, controls saddle and bridle, and corrects the rider's seat. The horse is led on from the right and taken on the right rein. As a rule, the first half of the lesson takes place on the left rein and the second half on the right.

When the rider has become accustomed to the trot and is able to sit quietly while holding on to the saddle, he may try to take his hand off the cantle first and later off the pommel. He should be able to remain in the saddle without being unbalanced by the horse's movement. If he is not able to maintain his seat it is far better to hold on again than to slip about in the saddle and disturb the horse's balance. It cannot be said too often that only the correct seat allows the horse to move in balance. When sitting independently the rider can apply the aids correctly, but he is unable to do so when struggling for his own balance in the saddle.

When the seat is sufficiently firm and the rider able to maintain his balance without holding on to the saddle, various exercises should be practiced to improve his suppleness and prevent stiffness. They will also increase the pupil's confidence in the horse. The teacher should take care that during these exercises the seat, thighs, and knees remain on the saddle as is required for the correct position. These exercises are meant to make the muscles relax, to obtain the necessary suppleness, and to improve balance. With young riders who have had little or no contact with horses so far, these exercises may be developed into gymnastics which will help them to find better contact with their partner. They will also make them more confident and bring a gay note into the more or less monotonous lessons on the longe. The teacher should remember, however, that this kind of gymnastics is only a means to reach a goal, that is, to obtain a firm, upright, and supple position in the saddle. He should never lose sight of this aim and allow the lesson to degenerate into a series of exercises which are of no value if executed in an incorrect position and with legs clinging to the horse like a pair of tongs.

The following exercises may be practiced on the longe: swinging arms forward and back; bending the upper part of the body forward and backward; turning the body; turning the head; swinging the lower legs back and forward; and circling the feet.

Bending the upper part backward until the back of the head touches the horse's hind quarters leads us to the gymnastic exercises which are called "voltige" and are not discussed in this book. A detailed description of these exercises on horseback may be found in *The Complete Training of Horse and Rider*.

Frequent transitions from the walk into the trot and vice versa are another means to improve the correct and firm seat. They should be brought about with suppleness and smoothness without the horse getting excited, as should be expected from any riding horse. If these transitions are executed calmly —calmness being the first requirement of a longe horse— they will prepare the rider for work at the canter, which may begin when, but never before, the rider can maintain a firm seat at an energetic trot without holding on to the saddle. Progress obtained so far may be annihilated by the canter when attempted too soon and, therefore, it should be begun as systematically as the work at the trot. Let us not forget that in these first lessons the confidence of the pupil in his horse and in himself is to be built up. For this reason the teacher must take care that the young rider is not thrown off in the beginning. Also he should remember that the canter is more tiring for a novice and ask only short periods to avoid fatigue.

There is a rule governing not only work on the longe but also the entire training up to the advanced stages: the teacher must bring the different exercises to an end before the pupil shows signs of fatigue, which is detrimental to the training. Periods at the walk interspersed in the lesson will give a rest to horse and rider and are accepted as a reward by both. In his eagerness to obtain progress the teacher might forget that these periods of rest and reward are necessary to prevent horse and rider from becoming stale and listless.

At the canter the teacher should insist that the pupil maintain his seat as correctly as at the walk and trot. He should not slide back and forth in the saddle and swing his lower legs, especially the inside one, nor adopt a stiff position.

Progress in both trot and canter will be obtained gradually —according to the talent of the pupil—by constantly correcting the seat. When the rider can control his body in all paces without ever holding on to the saddle, he may be taught the correct position of arms and hands and how to handle the reins.

The upper arms should hang freely from the shoulder and along the upper part of the body. The elbows should neither stick out nor be pressed against the body. The lower arms should be almost at right angles with the upper arms. The hands should be formed into a fist and held at the same level in front of the middle of the body, and slightly bent toward the body at the wrists. The reins are taken in both hands as already described earlier in this chapter and slightly applied. They must not be taken too long, which would induce the rider to stick his elbows out or lean his body behind the vertical. The hands with the thumbs uppermost are carried with a rounded wrist as close to each other as possible and at the same level, approximately one or two hands above the withers of the horse. They should be held neither too high, which would make them unsteady, nor too low with the back of the hand upward or even leaning on the horse's neck, which would make the rider's hand hard and render correct guidance impossible. It is important for the teacher to see that both hands are at equal distance from the horse's neck. The pupil must not be allowed to neck rein, that is, take his hand across the horse's neck to the opposite side.

In this last period of longeing the pupil is made familiar with guiding the horse himself. Longe and whip of the teacher will now be employed only when correcting or helping to push forward. The side reins should be made very long or even taken off altogether. Now the teacher commands the pace and speed which the student should demand from his horse while taking care to maintain his position and his seat. When increasing the speed or passing from the trot into the canter, his upper part must not fall back or lean forward when pace or speed is decreased. When controlling these exercises the instructor explains the influence of the upper part as an aid. Taking the body back pushes the horse forward, while leaning slightly forward helps to decrease the speed.

The teacher explains that the aids of the legs must always be given with a low heel. The leg applied on the girth pushes the horse forward, while applied behind the girth it will make him go sideways or, according to the intensity of the aid, will prevent him from swinging his hind quarters to this side.

Working on the longe in this way will increase the pupil's understanding and skill, which will be of great help later when he rides his own horse. The daily lesson on the longe should not exceed thirty to forty-five minutes. The entire time of training on the longe depends on the pupil's progress. Having obtained the independent seat is proof that he is ready for further training wherein he learns to guide his horse in the various paces and exercises without the longe.

It is not easy to determine the exact moment; with talented riders it may be reached after four to six weeks on the longe; with others, after several months. The instructor must be guided by this principle: in case of doubt he should continue to train the pupil on the longe for a longer period. The advantage of improving and confirming the seat outweighs the time spent on it, which is in any case never wasted.

I want to stress once more that these instructions are to give the pupil a sound foundation from which to continue even to advanced training and serious equestrian activity. The training on the longe is recommended not only for pupils who sit on a horse for the first time but also for those who need to correct a faulty position.

B. ON A RIDING HORSE

Not every riding teacher has a qualified longe horse at his disposal. However, any riding horse should be suitable for longeing lessons. The training as such follows the instructions already described, but the beginning will vary according to the horse available. At first the horse must be taught to go on the longe without the rider, which should not take longer than two or three days and will help to prevent unpleasant incidents for a novice rider on a horse unfamiliar with the longe. The horse comes into the arena with saddle, bridle, cavesson, and side reins. He is made to stand in the center of the circle on which he will be longed, and the side reins are attached to the rings of the snaffle. The stirrups remain pulled up since the rider does not mount yet. Either the teacher or the pupil leads the horse onto the circle on the left rein which, as we've said, is more familiar to him and on which he will understand more quickly.

Care must be taken so that he remains at a quiet walk and takes contact with the longe which plays the role of the reins. Should he try to run away he is to be brought to reason by shaking the longe and calling "Waaalk!" If he takes off repeatedly, the side reins should be shortened. When the horse stops he must be led on again calmly but not pushed forward with the whip. If he continues to stop, the side reins should be made longer. The longe is held in the left hand when the horse goes on the left rein and in the right when he goes on the right rein. The whip is held in the hand nearest to the horse. (See page 72.)

When the horse has gone for a few rounds at a quiet walk he is asked to trot by the voice, a click of the tongue, and by gently lifting the whip. Most riding horses will respond to the word "Trot!" said in a commanding tone of voice. Should he not react, the instructor lifts the whip and drops the lash to the ground behind the horse, or he takes a quicker step toward him. When there is still no reaction, the lash of the whip is applied gently, just dropped as if by its own weight against the same spot just behind the girth where the rider will use his leg aids later. The whip must never be used on the hind quarters or the hind legs, which would induce the horse to kick. When using the whip the teacher should repeat the word "Trot!" to make the horse familiar with his voice.

Horses have very keen hearing and take a sharp tone of voice as an encouragement or as a reprimand and soft and gentle sounds as calming and a reward. Young horses that are gay and naughty may be brought to reason when shouted at. The good hearing will also be of help in the training when the same words and the same tone of voice are used for the same demands.

The horse should move quietly at the trot. The trainer reduces the speed by gently shaking the longe. The whip instead of the leg aids is used as just described to make the horse go forward. When the horse submits willingly to the commands, the same procedure is repeated on the right rein. In case of difficulties they should be patiently dealt with as on the left rein.

When preparing the horse for the longeing lesson the teacher should ask the pupil to watch him and even to assist. It will give him an idea about longeing which might be helpful on later occasions. Besides he has an opportunity to get to know the horse and become familiar with his character and temperament. When the horse goes quietly and evenly on both reins on the longe, the pupil may mount and the lessons continue in the same way as described earlier in this chapter.

The lesson on the longe, for beginners as well as for more advanced pupils, should be brought to an end by two or three rounds at a quiet walk just as it should begin at this pace. Then the teacher faces the horse and takes him into the center by gently shortening the longe and calling "Come here." He brings him to a halt and makes him stand still. He pats him and asks the pupil to dismount. Leaning on his hands on the flaps of the saddle, the rider swings his legs backwards over the horse's back, vaulting off to the left side of the horse. The side reins are unclasped and joined over the horse's withers, and the girth is loosened, which the horse will accept as a reward. If stirrups were used they are pulled up and secured. The pupil, too, rewards his horse by patting him and giving him sugar and leads him back into the stables either by the longe and the cavesson or, if the longe has been removed, by the reins which have been passed forward over the horse's head.

In the last stage of training on the longe, the pupil may at the end of the lesson go a few times around the arena at a walk without the longe and with the side reins made very long or even removed altogether. This will give him a feeling of independence and prepare him for guiding his horse himself. Also he will feel that he has made progress in his training and increase his confidence in the horse.

The problems the instructor faces when longeing a beginner on an untrained horse are discussed on pages 62–67.

7. How to teach beginners in a group

When trying to form an opinion about the present state of the sport of riding, it is necessary to consider it retrospectively in order to understand what goes on in most riding schools today.

For centuries riding was influenced by the military and the horse was a vital part of everyday life. The army trained and maintained a sufficient number of teachers and trainers who were responsible for the standard of riding and the maintenance of the horses. Their influence on the civilian riding sport was unmistakable. Technical progress has now eliminated the horse from the army almost completely. Contrary to this development, the interest in riding has broadened in an unforeseen way. The growing multitude of riders and riding enthusiasts, however, is facing an ever-decreasing number of qualified instructors. This fact will not fail to mark the standard of the sport of riding and actually does make itself felt already even in the spheres of advanced training.

Therefore, the conscientious basic training as described in the previous chapters will not be available to all young riders, for the instructor is not able to concentrate exclusively on one pupil. Lessons in a group are necessarily given greater importance. There is nothing new about them, since in the cavalry soldiers were always drilled in a group.

It must be underlined, though, that lessons in a group cannot give the foundation necessary to participate successfully in competitions. Observing his group carefully, the teacher may detect a talented rider after a while and concentrate especially on him. Most pupils, on the other hand, have no other ambition than to be able to sit in the saddle and take their horses out on rides. These demands may be easily fulfilled by lessons in a group. Here the rider may learn how to sit and to guide his horse. The degree of his achievements will be a more modest one compared with training on the longe, and the part of the horse as the assistant of the teacher is also of lesser importance.

In this stage the teacher should not take more than three to eight pupils at a time in a group. Also, they should be approximately of the same standard. If not, it might happen that more advanced students may find the modest demands tedious (which should not be the case, as the consolidation of the foundation should be welcome at any time and will always bear fruit later), or inexperienced pupils might be discouraged by demands exceeding their capabilities. The horses, too, should be on the same level of training and follow a lead horse going one behind the other in the ring. They should not require much guidance so the teacher can concentrate on the seat of his pupils. One of the students who is able to ride his horse forward on straight lines at the walk and at the trot is asked to head the group.

The beginning of the lesson is the same as described in the previous chapters. The horse must be accustomed to going in a school ring. The pupils should saddle their own horses, take them into the arena in a snaffle and with side reins, and line them up on the center line parallel to the short side of the school, leaving enough distance between them. An open arena should be fenced in; marking it with letters or symbols is not sufficient in the present case. The teacher decides the length of the side reins, which varies according to the temperament and the character of each horse. With a calm horse the side reins should be long enough to allow him to take a light contact. An excited animal will be prevented from running away by shorter side reins. When the horse has a tendency to carry his head too high, the side reins should be fastened lower into the girth; they should be fastened higher with a horse that carries his head and neck too low. The point is not, however, to press the horse into a determined position by means of the side reins but to maintain his form and keep him under control even under an inexperienced rider who has as yet little or no influence on his horse. The horses should remain quietly at a standstill (required of any good riding horse!) while the pupils mount and the teacher controls their seat. He determines the order in which to follow the first rider and gives the commands regarding which rein to move on at a walk.

It may happen in the beginning that some of the pupils are not able to make their horses move into the demanded direction. The teacher should calmly take the cheek strap and lead the horse to his place in the row. It would be absolutely wrong to make him obey by using the whip or shouting at the pupil. The teacher should remember how utterly helpless the ignorant beginner is with his horse and not give way to impatience. In the group the riders should observe a distance of three steps from each other, which allows the teacher to take them in at a glance. It may be necessary to push forward with the whip those horses that lag behind, but the whip should only be raised behind the horse and not used on him. If this is not sufficient, the side reins should be lengthened. They should be shortened with those horses that close up too much behind the rider in front of them. Following their herding instinct the horses will in a few days go in the group and maintain the distance from each other.

Now the riding instructor concentrates on the correct seat of his pupils, not trying, however, to obtain everything at the same time and giving preference to the most important. First he makes the rider sit in the center of the saddle and place his legs flat along the body of the horse with a low heel and a firm grip of the knee. From the very beginning he must not allow his pupils to ride with their knees turned to the outside, pulling their heels up and with the calves clamped to the horse, as may be seen so often. This fault must be nipped in the bud, as it is very difficult to eliminate later on. How would a rider give the correct leg aids when glued to the horse with calves and heels?

The next step is to teach the position of the upper part of the body, which should be upright with the shoulders taken back but not stiff. Only a supple body can follow the horse's movements. The carriage of the head is closely related to the position of the body. The chin should be drawn back and the eyes directed forward over the ears of the horse. As already mentioned, looking down encourages the rider to round his back. Equally faulty is leaning back or forward.

The pupils have to be constantly reminded of these faults, for while concentrating on one thing the young rider is likely to forget the rest of them. Here the instructor may give evidence of his qualities as a teacher and prove his patience as he repeats these corrections until progress becomes visible. There will be no result when he shouts at his pupils and uses bad language—a negative heritage come down from army drill to our riding schools. It is the advantage of riding in a group that all pupils can hear these corrections, and serious and ambitious riders will try to look for the same fault in themselves. Of course, any progress should by all

54

means be mentioned and the pupil praised whenever appropriate.

During the first lessons the group rides mainly at a walk and only for very short periods at the trot (not more than one long side of the arena). Then, with the exception of the first rider, all pupils shorten the reins by making a knot and placing them on the horse's neck. No longer obliged to guide their horses, they can concentrate entirely on practicing the correct seat. Gymnastic exercises may be interspersed to increase the suppleness of the riders and their confidence in the horse. These exercises are similar to those explained in the chapter about the training on the longe. Again it should be emphasized that they are only a means to obtain a supple seat and not the object of the lesson.

When the beginners have become familiar with their new activity, the working trot may be ridden for longer periods. The working trot is a speed between collected and ordinary trot and is practiced for training purposes only. Here the pupil faces new problems, as we've seen in the training on the longe. To begin with, these periods at the trot should not exceed one or two times around the arena and be repeated in the following days—if there are no difficulties—and extended for longer duration until there is as much work at the trot as there is at the walk. At this stage the pupils may lay the stirrup leathers crosswise over their horses' necks and ride temporarily without stirrups.

Toward the end of the lesson the pupils should take up the reins while the teacher controls and corrects the position of hands and arms. It is most important that right from the beginning the pupils adopt the habit of guiding their horses with a quiet and elastic hand which allows the horse to take a light and steady contact on the bit. After three or four weeks the students should guide their horses independently throughout the lesson. For repeated corrections of the seat they may occasionally place the reins over the horse's neck.

Once again I want to underline that in this stage of training the main goal is to make the pupil familiar with the horse and to teach him the correct seat. It would be absolutely wrong and proof of false ambition to demand any exercises or figures from these beginners. It should not be forgotten that it does not matter so much what exercises the rider shows but how he executes them. Besides, the pupils of such groups have generally no other aim than to go for a ride for their pleasure. They need a firm seat, without which they would be thrown whenever there was a disturbance, and they must be able to guide their horses in the desired direction. Also, they should present a pleasant sight on horseback, which will result from the cultivation of the correct seat and which will make them worthy representatives of the "noblest of all sports."

According to these requirements, the period of training will take about four to six weeks—corresponding to the talent of the pupils—and be brought to an end by teaching the rising trot and the canter. It is a mistake to demand the rising trot at the speed of the working trot, which would result in unrhythmical and unsightly movements of the rider. Whether in the arena or cross-country, the rising trot is practiced at an ordinary speed only. The rider rides on the outside diagonal, that is, on the right rein he rises from the saddle when the right hind leg and the left foreleg come off the ground and he sits down when the same diagonal returns to the ground. In other words, it is the inside hind leg which receives the rider's weight. From the movement of the horse's shoulder the rider can decide in which moment to sit down or to rise. In this case, riding to the right, he sits when the horse lowers his left shoulder.

Before the first canter the teacher explains the aids for

the strike-off. To begin with he should ask one pupil at a time to try the canter while the others continue at the trot. He helps the first rider by pushing the horse forward with the whip and calling "Hop!" The pupil strikes off into the canter from the trot when passing the first corner of the short side of the arena. Thus he has the chance of a second try in the next corner if his attempt fails. He canters around the arena and takes his horse into a trot again when coming up behind the last rider of the group. At that moment the rider in front of the group, in turn, strikes off into the canter. This method gives the teacher the opportunity to concentrate on one rider at a time and to interfere if necessary. Should a horse run away, the fault is to be sought with the teacher. He has made the fundamental mistake of asking the canter too soon. Now he must try to bring the horse to reason by calling him, by calming him with his voice. He may try to block his way but then risks provoking a fall for the rider. It is no credit to the teacher if he shouts at the unfortunate student. Rather, he should remind him to take his upper part back, as rolling himself into a ball makes it easier for the horse to throw his rider. Neither should the pupil hold onto the reins for dear life, but by a giving and taking action try to get the horse under his control. At any rate, the other riders should bring their horses immediately to a walk to avoid a general rodeo. Walk and trot should be practiced during the following few days until the canter is repeated again with great care. The canter should not be practiced by the entire group until every rider has his horse under his control and is able to maintain an even speed and an even distance from the horse in front. In general the group should not canter for more than two to three rounds. The horses should not become excited by the canter. As by the movement of the horse the pupil slides to the outside, the teacher must constantly remind him to sit on the inside seat bone.

Such lessons in a group require school horses of approximately the same standard of training. They should go in the three basic paces, walk, trot, and canter and by all means have a quiet temperament. The riders should be able to meet at determined hours of the day, for the coming and going of riders within the group makes instruction very difficult and slows down a progressive program of training.

8. When the instructor provides the horse

Occasionally the teacher decides to use his own horse for the training of a pupil. This is the case when the teacher not only gives lessons but also schools his own horses and participates in competitions in order to prove the correctness of his method and broaden his knowledge. There is no doubt that this kind of activity will convey to him new impulse and experience for his work. He may also break in and train young horses and sell them when they have reached a certain standard of training. The demand for well-trained horses is universally great and by far exceeds the number available. (In this book we deal mainly with dressage horses; the situation with jumpers is entirely different.)

A riding teacher who offers his own horse for instruction will choose his pupil with great care and hardly give his horse to a beginner, unless he plans to sell him the horse as soon as the pupil has made sufficient progress. When taking active part in competitive sport—which adds considerably to his reputation as a teacher—he may temporarily lend his horse to an advanced pupil but hardly ever use him as a longe horse. It should not be forgotten that a horse advanced in dressage is spoiled much more quickly than a jumper.

On the other hand, having trained the horse himself and knowing him thoroughly allows the teacher a much more individual way of instruction. Being familiar with all strong and weak points of his "assistant," he derives advice and correction from his personal experience. The student has the great chance to feel how a well-trained horse should move and react to his aids. Such instruction, when made available to a talented and serious pupil, may be of invaluable influence on his career as a rider. It is important, however, that the teacher should ride his horse at regular intervals in order to maintain his standard of training and eradicate faults which may be expected to appear under a less knowledgeable rider. This aspect and the fact that apart from the progress of his pupil the teacher wants to bring his horse along will make this sort of instruction less continuous than when the pupil rides his own horse or a school horse. These disadvantages are not always outweighed by the benefits mentioned above. In any event, the lessons should follow the pattern described in the following chapters.

9. A beginner on his own (green) horse

Sometimes the instructor is faced with the situation of teaching a beginner who has never been on a horse before but who owns one. There are parents who believe that the main thing is to buy a horse for the child and that learning to ride will follow automatically. The same problem may arise with adults. The innocent buyer is often taken in by a crafty dealer who, taking advantage of his ignorance and praising the exquisite qualities of a particular horse, sells him without even showing him under the rider. As trained horses fetch enormous prices nowadays they are easy to undercut and yet make a profit. And then the beginner owns a horse that is still very young and hardly broken in.

In this case the teacher should by all means ride the horse

and determine his temperament and his standard of training before planning his lessons. It would be advantageous to ask the opinion of the teacher before buying a horse. He might try out the horse in question and advise the prospective owner as to his conformation, schooling, and price. Regardless of his standard of training, the horse is first to be used on the longe to teach the beginner a correct seat and make him understand the basic rules of riding. Even an untrained horse with a quiet temperament may be suitable for that.

Now the instructor must teach both horse and rider at the same time. There are pros and cons to every system. In this case it is an advantage that the pupil not only learns a correct seat on the longe but at the same time observes how to deal with a green horse and how to longe him, which is of great benefit for every rider. On the other hand, the training will take at least twice as long as on an experienced school horse.

At first the teacher should help his pupil to make his horse familiar with the different surroundings, a new stable, other horses, and new people. This is all the more important if the pupil takes care of his horse himself. But even when there are grooms the beginner should be around his horse, especially with a young one or one that comes from pasture, and not leave him entirely to the groom. Apart from the fact that there is a shortage of knowledgeable grooms, it helps the young rider to become familiar with his horse. The importance of the relationship between horse and rider has been mentioned repeatedly.

Care, saddling, and bridling will follow the instructions given on pages 25–30. With a young horse that is not broken in, the instructor will proceed even more carefully in order to gain the confidence of the young animal. He should be walked for two or three days, preferably out of doors, before introducing him to saddle and bridle. Thus he becomes accustomed to being constantly under the control of man.

When bridling a young horse for the first time, the teacher should be very careful to proceed very slowly and talk to the horse. He must not become afraid of the bit, which might be the cause of many difficulties later on. Again, the most important thing is to gain his confidence.

The saddle is best fitted in the stables where the horse is under better control than outside. As described on pages 27–29, care must be taken that the saddle does not touch the withers and is placed on the horse's back in such a way that the girths which hold it lie on the true ribs. To begin with, the girth is left very loose, just tight enough to prevent the saddle from slipping. For a few more days the horse is walked with the saddle while the girths are tightened gradually hole by hole until they are sufficiently tight to hold the saddle for the rider to mount. Tightening the girth too much or too quickly might cause uneasiness in the horse and induce him to blow himself up. This bad habit, once established, is very difficult to eliminate. He might also throw himself on the ground or stand up on his hind legs and fall over backwards. In the initial stage of training, all precautions should be taken to prevent the horse from becoming conscious of his strength and finding means and ways to evade the authority of man.

Now the horse is taken for a walk of half an hour at least with saddle and bridle and cavesson and on the longe. It is advisable to lead the horse with a cavesson and a longe, as they permit a better control over him, especially if he gets frightened or jumps about, without jerking his mouth. According to his temperament he should be walked without a rider for about three to six days altogether. There is ample opportunity during this time to observe him, study his character, and lay the foundation of confidence. When the horse goes quietly, the young rider may lead him while feeding him titbits.

When the horse behaves well and seems to begin to understand what is expected of him, he is brought into the arena to be longed as explained on page 48. Those procedures are here complemented by instructions necessary for a completely green horse. The side reins are fastened to the girth and the correct length adjusted so that there is practically no influence on the snaffle bit to which the young horse must yet grow accustomed. The instructor clasps the longe into the cavesson and asks the pupil to lead the horse on the left rein at a walk, describing a circle around the teacher. The pupil holds the cheek strap with his right hand and the whip in his left, directed toward the ground and not toward the horse, which might irritate or frighten him. When the horse has gone a few rounds at a quiet walk, the pupil lets go of the bridle and remains next to the horse for another round. Should he try to take off, the right hand takes hold of the cheek strap without pulling and brings the horse to reason. The horse will understand quickly and remain at a quiet walk. Now the pupil walks slowly away from the horse along the longe and stands beside the teacher, who holds the longe. He takes the whip in the right hand, which is nearest to the horse.

Should the horse try to follow the pupil or come to a standstill, he is led on again calmly. On no account should he be pushed forward or out onto the circle with the whip. Should he rush off, he is taken into the center of the circle with the longe, or if this fails, the pupil stands with his arms spread on the circle blocking the horse's path and bringing him to standstill. No horse would run down a person in such a case.

When treated with patience and understanding, the horse will soon comprehend and go willingly on the longe. In the beginning of the lesson he should go at a walk, but should he break into a quiet trot he may remain in this pace for a while and be taken calmly into a walk again later on. Speaking to the horse is important—it will calm him and make him confident. After a while, short periods at the trot should be interspersed. Changes of pace and the transitions help to get better control over the horse, who should not be allowed to choose the pace or speed he pleases.

When the horse goes willingly on the left rein, work on the right rein may begin. Here difficulties may occur with a young horse; they should be dealt with quietly and in the same manner as on the left rein (as explained before, horses are used to being led from the left).

From the beginning and throughout the entire training, care must be taken not to overwork a young horse. While working on the longe, the circle should be as large as possible, at least sixteen meters in diameter. The smaller the circle, the more strenuous the work for the horse. Also, changes of rein should be made frequently. In general, the horse should not be trotted for more than five minutes in the beginning and have a period of rest at the walk before another trot. When the horse keeps an even speed (tempo) and willingly obeys the commands of the trainer, the side reins may gradually be shortened. This will teach the horse to adopt the correct position of the head, which will help him to carry his rider with an arched back. Should he try to raise his head and neck too much and carry his nose high, he would feel the rider's weight uncomfortably on his back. This would have a bad influence on his physical development also. In this case the side reins are fastened at a lower point into the girth. If he carries his head too low, shifting his weight onto the forehand, the side reins are clasped into the girth just below the buckle or even in a ring on the front of the saddle.

When the young horse has become accustomed to going

on the longe at the walk and trot and the transitions are made willingly, the trainer may begin the canter. It will be easiest for the horse to understand the strike-off if the instructor somewhat shortens the speed at the trot and takes the horse onto a smaller circle. Pushing him forward with the whip pointing to the girth and making him go back on the circle will make the horse strike off into the canter and do so on the correct leg. In addition the trainer calls "Hop!" or gives a click of the tongue. After two or three rounds at the canter, the horse is taken back into a trot and walk, brought to a halt, and rewarded. In a short while, calling "Hop!" will be sufficient to induce the horse to strike off. Should he strike off on the wrong lead, he is quietly taken into a trot again and the attempt repeated. It may take some time until the horse has understood. In this case he must be rewarded immediately by calling "Good!" and taken into the walk after a few rounds. The voice should change in tone and modulation to make the horse understand the difference between reward and reprimand. On the longe a young horse is always made to strike off from the trot.

The moment for mounting has come when the horse remains obedient and calm in all paces and transitions from one pace to the other, which may be expected after three to six weeks, according to the age of the horse. Mounting, too, should be undertaken with great care and calmness to prevent the horse from being startled and frightened. Before mounting, the rider should slap the saddle on both sides with the flat of his hand several times to make the horse used to noise coming from this direction. Then an assistant (the groom, for instance) should lift the pupil up to the saddle where he remains propped on his hands with both legs on the left side of the horse. When the horse remains quiet, after a while he swings his right leg high over the horse's back and lowers himself gently into the saddle. The horse should be given oats or titbits by the teacher to make him stand still, divert his attention, and reward him. As a rule the young horse should not be made to stand still for too long. Then the pupil takes the stirrups and work may begin at the walk as explained on pages 41–44.

The further training continues in the same manner as described before, with the exception that in this case progress will be slower, since both horse and rider have to learn at the same time. The horse must learn to understand his trainer, and must learn to move with regularity and in balance, which may be obtained with the gradual development of his muscles. These circumstances have to be considered when deciding the duration of the various periods of work. Fatigue is to be strictly avoided, as it slows down progress. Suppleness, which the young and green horse lacks, must be built up by the daily training. This lack of suppleness makes it more difficult for the young rider to sit correctly than it would be on a well-trained horse. Great patience is necessary on the part of the teacher, though he has better control over horse and rider on the longe than when having a beginner on a green horse in a group of other riders. Before beginning with gymnastic exercises, the horse should be made accustomed to the rider's weight shifting in the saddle and to movements above his head. Preferably at the walk, the pupil slowly lifts one arm while holding on to the saddle with the other hand. When the horse has become used to these movements and does not change in his action or alter the position of his head, further exercises at the various paces may be demanded.

There is one important fact that the teacher must not lose sight of. In the chapter about work on the longe, attention was drawn to the fact that the beginner should find his balance on his horse in movement and that the walk and a shortened trot were best suited and easiest for the rider to sit. The young horse on the longe will soon understand this trot with short relaxed steps and even realize that it is more comfortable for him. But what is easier for the rider and more comfortable for the horse is in this case not the best means to a proper training of the four-legged partner. Learning to go forward and in balance with his rider demands much impulsion, which the horse does not gain when trotting leisurely. On the other hand, the beginner is not able to sit through an energetic trot for long and soon will disturb the horse's balance by bumping and slipping in the saddle. This will in turn hinder the horse's urge to go forward. As a consequence he becomes increasingly reluctant to go forward, which has a negative influence on his further training and eventually makes him lose his paces. Therefore, once or twice a week the teacher should longe the horse without the rider and make him go forward at an energetic trot to build up the necessary impulsion and at the same time increase suppleness before continuing with the training of the rider.

It is particularly necessary to longe the horse without the rider when by his increasing reluctance to go forward he begins to lose his impulsive paces. This reluctance is caused by the unskilled rider and becomes especially obvious when the horse performs short and hasty steps instead of longer ones when asked to increase the speed. This is absolutely contrary to what should be obtained by work on the longe. The instructor should take it as a serious warning and continue to longe the horse without the rider and make him go well forward until he has eliminated a setback which would be detrimental to the entire training. The duration for which regular work is to be interrupted depends on how soon the teacher has become aware of the fault. Correction will take the longer the later he has detected the setback. Although proceeding in this manner slows down the course of training, in the interest of both horse and rider this time is not wasted.

When the rider has acquired a firm seat and the horse obediently follows the demands of the teacher's voice, whip, and longe, the pupil may take up the reins and begin to guide his horse, at first, on the longe. The teacher should warn him not to hold on to the reins to re-establish his lost balance. The side reins are gradually lengthened until they have no more effect and the horse takes contact with the hand of the rider. Should the horse raise his head and drop his back, although he had adopted the correct position of his head with the side reins adjusted, either the hand of the pupil is too hard or the horse is not yet ready for this new stage of training. The only true remedy is to shorten the side reins to their original length and continue to work on the rider's independent seat until the desired result may be obtained.

When the rider is able to guide his horse independently of his teacher, who uses the longe only when necessary, he should learn to apply the leg aids correctly. When the rider's aids are too weak or fail to be effective, the teacher helps by using the whip, that is, by showing it to the horse or dropping the lash to the ground. Frequent transitions into the trot and the walk help to improve the skill of the pupil as well as the attention of the horse. Strike-off into the canter may also be practiced with the assistance of the teacher's voice if the transitions from the walk into the trot and vice versa succeed well. At this stage of training, the pupil may ride a few times around the arena at a walk before dismounting. The instructor walks near the horse's head, holding him loosely on the longe and being immediately at hand in case of difficulties. At last, at the end of the lesson, the pupil is allowed to ride around without the longe and later without the side reins. The lesson is brought to an end in the same pattern as described on pages 50–51.

10. *How to build up the lessons methodically and logically*

A. ON A SCHOOL HORSE

When a rider has acquired the fundamental notions of riding and has proved talented for further training, systematic schooling may begin. While so far he has been a mere passenger on his horse, now he will learn to guide and work him and eventually even school him himself. It is understood that he has learned to sit independently in all movements of his horse and use hands and legs to give the aids and not to maintain his seat in the saddle.

Should this section of training be taught in a group, it is essential that the riders be at the same level of training and able to assemble always at the same time. We have mentioned the disadvantages of teaching a group of pupils in different stages of training. The school horses, too, should be of equal standard. Whether given to a single student or to several riders, the instruction will follow a certain line and aim for the same result. The difference is for the teacher who, instead of having a single pupil, has to supervise several at the same time, which makes instruction lose intensity. As pointed out in the chapter about longeing, it is impossible to correct all faults at once. Neither can the teacher concentrate on all pupils at the same time. This disadvantage is outweighed by the fact that in a group the horses stimulate each other to go forward, while the single student has to produce impulsion himself by the pushing aids and teach his horse the forward urge.

The program of work will vary according to the horse available, that is, whether the lessons are given on a trained school horse, on a horse that has gone on the longe most of the time, or even on a young horse.

With the trained school horse, teacher and pupil are given

68

a four-legged assistant that will make the young rider understand the correct administration of the aids and their intensity and convey to him the feeling of movement in correct balance. Here the foundation is laid for the understanding that will enable him to school young horses much later when he has gained experience along with knowledge and physical skill. By theoretical studies he should complement his knowledge and understanding. Among other things, theory comprises a thorough knowledge of the anatomy and physiology of the animal. What, from lack of time, cannot be passed on to him by his teacher, the pupil should acquire from literature on the subject.

The lesson begins with mounting. When building up the training on a solid foundation, the teacher should not presume any knowledge in his pupil and always be prepared to return to very basic instruction. The horse is led into the school ring and mounted as described in the chapter about longeing. The rider mounts on the center line parallel to the short side. The instructor controls his pupil and immediately corrects any faults. Correction does not mean shouting, of course, but a calm explanation. The teacher should insist that the horse stand still and on all four legs during the process of mounting and until asked to move on by the rider. Fidgeting on the spot or moving on without command must not be tolerated. This fundamental principle cannot be mentioned too often.

At the standstill the rider's seat is controlled and if necessary corrected. Together with the correct seat the correct carriage and use of the whip is to be explained. As with everything else in riding, it should be both practical and elegant. Because details are often neglected these days we find many deviations from the rule which in no way contribute to a rider's appearance. When riding in a snaffle, the whip should always be carried in the inside hand, that is, in the hand that is turned toward the center of the ring. It is held at the end and across the rider's thigh so that it points toward the horse's flank. From the correct carriage of the whip the teacher can judge the position of the rider's hands. Only when the hands are carried in the correct way with the thumbs uppermost as described on pages 40–41, "Training on the longe," can the whip be carried correctly and used effectively. When saluting, the reins and the whip must be in the left hand and the hat is doffed with the right. There are unfortunately many variations of a rider's salute to be seen in public and in horse shows.

Having controlled the rider's seat at a standstill and given the necessary commands for the lesson, the teacher asks the pupil to set his horse in motion at a walk and with the reins applied. He also tells him on which rein to continue after having reached the long side of the arena. When there are several pupils in a class, the order of riders is given beforehand and should be headed by the calmest horse. In case of difficulties which might happen to an inexperienced rider, it is of no avail to repeat the command, much less to shout at the unfortunate pupil. The teacher must tell him calmly in a few words what to do with reins and legs.

Along with the explanation of the aids to use, the teacher should concentrate on shaping and improving the rider's position and on maintaining the form of the horse. His remarks must be short and to the point, the riding school being no place for complicated explanations. He should focus his attention on his pupil and never mind the spectators. Too often the instructor gives his lesson less for the benefit of his pupil than for the sake of the audience, especially when there are friends or experts whom he wants to impress by long or presumably witty lectures. These are lost on the pupil who is unable to follow such long-winded explanations. He cannot even hear them, especially when riding away from his teacher.

There is many a rider, too, who is forever intent on catching the spectator's attention by executing all sorts of exercises while, working unwatched, he is quickly bored and at a loss what to do with his horse. Such showing off is a bad account of pupil and teacher alike. Moreover, the latter also risks losing his authority with his pupils.

During the first days the teacher should be satisfied when the horse goes willingly forward along the wall. The wall makes it easier for the horse to go straight and for the pupil to guide his horse. Holding the reins correctly is important for guiding the horse and must constantly be controlled by the instructor (see pages 40–42). Now the correct length of the reins has to be determined which allows the horse to take contact with the hands of the rider as he maintains the correct position in the saddle. The length of the reins depends on the length of the rider's lower arms. If the reins are too long the elbows will stick out or the rider lean back, his upper part coming behind the vertical and his seat behind the movement of the horse. Therefore, riders with long arms have shorter reins and carry their hands somewhat away from their body, while riders with short lower arms have longer reins and hold their hands closer to their body.

In the beginning of the lesson the horse should go along the wall for a few rounds at the walk and with loose reins. This is of great advantage as it gives him the opportunity after many hours in the stables to stretch and relax and calmly adjust to the rider's weight. This kind of warming up is the best way to take away the stiffness every horse feels after coming out of the stables, especially from a tie stall, which gives little possibility for movement. There is much talk of warming up before working, but it is not always done in an intelligent way. A horse cannot relax physically and mentally when being raced around at a trot or canter for the first ten minutes or more. Neither would an athlete loosen his muscles by a four-mile run but, rather, tire himself. Loosening exercises are the best preparation before beginning proper work.

Walk on the loose rein, which is the foundation of all other paces, helps the horse to find his physical and mental balance. The rider is given opportunity to adopt the correct seat in the saddle and the teacher can correct the pupil's position. Walk on the loose rein—that is, without taking contact—does not mean dragging along but advancing with long regular strides which the rider must demand from his horse by an occasional short leg aid on the girth with a low heel and the knee firmly on the saddle. This pushing aid should never degenerate into a constant kicking, which would blunt the horse's responsiveness and eventually fail to obtain any result at all. This might be compared with a person who is constantly shouted at. After a short while he will no longer react in any way but will remain unresponsive to any command.

If the horse does not react to the pushing aids of the pupil's legs, as may happen with an inexperienced rider who does not yet have much influence on his horse, the teacher may allow him to use the whip or may help with the longe whip himself. The pupil should apply the whip close behind his leg and, if this is not enough, tap the horse lightly on the same spot, taking great care not to give a jerk in the mouth with the rein at the same time. This would not only destroy the effect of the whip but also confuse and irritate the horse. The use of the longe whip was explained on page 49. It is important to remember that in this case the teacher must not use it as a punishment but to reinforce the pupil's leg aids.

When the horse has gone willingly several times around the arena at a regular walk on a loose rein and without getting hasty, the instructor gives the command to apply the reins and to trot. The rider should shorten the reins gradually and just enough to establish a light contact and so be able to guide his horse. He should never tighten the reins or hold on to them when losing balance. If the rider pulls at the reins, the horse will either lie on the bit or throw his head up. As this makes it more difficult for him to carry the rider, the horse will lose his balance. Consequently the rider can no longer maintain the correct seat. Such difficulties must be detected by the teacher in the beginning. It might even be necessary for him to mount himself and show the pupil how to apply the reins correctly and without disturbing the horse's contact. These first periods of trot are executed at the working trot in which the horse takes shorter strides than at the ordinary speed but not as short as in the collected trot. The rider sits through the movement as he did on the longe.

In the beginning the pupil should just take his horse calmly forward along the wall and execute the transitions from the walk to the trot and vice versa smoothly and without abruptness. The teacher controls the pupil's aids and warns him against seeking support in the reins or falling back with his upper part in the transition into the trot. Nor should the upper body fall forward when passing from the trot into the walk. The exact execution of these transitions is much more important for a sound foundation than riding all sorts of turns and circles improperly. When passing through the corners of the riding school a large curve is described, with care that speed and rhythm remain unaltered. The change of rein is best executed over the diagonal of the arena and, in the beginning, at the walk.

After a few days the ordinary trot is substituted for the working trot. Now the rising trot is practiced, as it is easier for the pupil to co-ordinate the balance of his seat with the movements of the horse in this speed. Besides, both horse and rider will find it easier to cultivate impulsion and the urge to go forward, which are necessary for progress for both. The rider rides on the outside diagonal, that is, once more, he rises from the saddle when the inside hind leg and the outside foreleg leave the ground and sits again when both legs return to the ground. Observations made in various

73

commercial riding schools cause me to underline again that it is impossible to ride a rising trot at the working tempo. This old rule is proved true by the caricatures presented by pupils whose teacher demands such absurdity. The unrhythmical twisting of their bodies in no way co-ordinates with the movements of the horse.

Again the teacher must remember in time to command a period of walk in order to prevent fatigue which would result in the pupil neglecting his seat and the horse losing impulsion and dragging his feet. Any demand made beyond strength and capability will make them stale and listless and undermine the pupil's confidence in the teacher as well as that of the horse in the rider. Lacking the gift of language, the horse expresses by his behavior if and when too much has been demanded. Therefore, the instructor must concentrate entirely and continuously on horse and rider. It is not enough to set up a schedule of time for the various exercises; he has to observe his pupils throughout the whole lesson. By having an exact notion of the physical and mental dispositions of both horse and rider, trying to think from the pupil's standpoint, and passing on his personal experience, he will best find the individual way of proceeding which will take him on the straightest path to success.

As a preparation for further work and for increased impulsion, it is advisable to alternate the rising trot at the ordinary speed with a few strides at the sitting trot. This will introduce the pupil gradually to more advanced work which is done mainly at the sitting trot. Moreover, the rider's feeling for the trot is thus cultivated. With the alternated rising and sitting trot the teacher must insist that the horse maintain an even tempo as well as impulsion and forward urge, and that he not lose the regular rhythm by taking too strong a contact on the bit. When performed correctly this exercise proves the progress of the mental and physical balance of horse and rider.

When the pupil has learned to ride straight forward along the wall and in light contact, maintaining the correct seat and correct guidance, the next step is to present his horse in proper shape. This is best practiced on the circle, where it is easier to preserve the form of the horse. Also, the teacher can observe his pupil better in all phases of the movement and administer his corrections promptly. He should not always remain in the center of the circle but now and again stand on the outside. From this vantage point he can see whether the rider sits exactly in the middle of the saddle, or whether he lifts his outside shoulder, which would collapse his inside hip. The same fault appears when the rider's seat is made to slide to the outside by the movements of the horse and he attempts to sit upright on this displaced base. The position of the outside leg is controlled from outside the circle; it should be placed slightly behind the girth with a low heel and prevent the hind quarters from swinging to the outside. The instructor should use the opportunity to explain the effect of the preventing leg. From within the circle the teacher makes sure that the pupil brings his outside shoulder sufficiently forward and that his inside leg remains quietly on the horse's body in all movements. Again the teacher applies his greatest attention to the rider's correct seat, which is necessary for the correct aids.

However, correcting the rider should not make the teacher forget to eliminate the faults of the horse. It is important that the circle be truly round and that the pupil be told the aids to be applied. The circle is a continuous turn and, therefore, well suited to teach the guidance of the horse in turns. In a turn the horse's spine is bent according to the arc of the circle, with the degree to which it is bent corresponding to the size of the circle. The increased flexion on

75

a small circle demands a greater effort on the part of the horse. So, it is easier for him to describe a larger circle (approximately twenty meters) which is preferable to a small one (twelve meters) incorrectly ridden. The teacher should watch critically to see that the horse does move on a true circle of regular size and does not make it smaller or larger according to his own will. He should warn the pupil of a frequent fault which occurs where the circle touches the walls of the riding school. The horse, to make work easier for himself, tries to go along the wall for three to four meters, thus interrupting the arc of the circle and at the same time the gymnastic effect of the exercise. Work on the circle is of great importance for the basic training of both horse and rider and the teacher should explain the necessary aids carefully and strictly demand their correct application.

On the circle the horse is guided with both reins. The inside rein holds the horse on the circle and determines the position of head and neck. It is of stronger effect than the outside rein, which defines the degree of the position as well as the size of the circle. Without the outside rein the horse would not bend in his body but just turn his head into the circle. The rider's inside leg is applied on the girth; it pushes the horse forward and bends him evenly from poll to tail. It is around the inside leg that the body of the horse is bent in its whole length according to the arc of the circle. It is for this reason that the inside leg is so important. In a turn it is more important than the aid of the inside rein. The outside leg is applied behind the girth, preventing the hind quarters from swinging to the outside and reinforcing the flexion of the horse's body around the inside leg. From the beginning the teacher should see that the horse's body is not bent more in the neck than in the whole body, which would interfere with the development of his movement and destroy the benefit of work on the circle.

76

The teacher should always remember that even the simple exercises are difficult for the beginner to perform and, therefore, gradually increase his demands as to correct seat and guidance of the horse in accordance with the growing skill and understanding of the pupil. When building up his lessons systematically he will have the opportunity to encourage his pupil with praise and make him take pleasure in riding. Increasing his demands too quickly, on the other hand, would force him to criticize too often, which would soon discourage the rider. When proceeding with psychological insight the teacher will adjust his demands to the individual and so find ample occasion to administer justified praise together with the necessary corrections. He should not try to correct all faults of his pupil at the same time, a mistake often committed by a mediocre instructor without psychological understanding. Too many corrections only confuse an inexperienced rider and make him tense, mentally and physically. Riding, however, wants both horse and rider to be completely relaxed and at ease. This relaxedness and ease reveals itself to the teacher as well as to the pupil in the smooth movements of the horse which allow the rider to sit quietly and without being bumped about in the saddle. The rider's relaxedness becomes obvious when he is able to maintain his seat with natural ease, when he feels his body move in harmony with the action of the horse, as he carries his hands quietly in front of his body and adopts the rhythm of the pace. Tenseness or ease is also mirrored in the expression on the face of the rider as well as on that of the horse. In this stage of training, as we've seen, it is necessary to concentrate on the form of the rider as well as on that of the horse. The teacher makes the pupil understand how he can maintain the correct form of the school horse and what fault he commits when losing it. The correct form of the horse is obtained by the judiciously balanced influence of the pushing (leg) and restraining (rein) aids. The performance of horse and rider should blend into one. When the horse moves correctly the rider is able to sit correctly in all movements. On the other hand, the ability of the rider is reflected in the way the horse moves. From the regularity of the horse's motion the teacher can judge the seat and the aids of his pupil. Already in this phase great importance should be attached to the fact that the few exercises that are demanded should be executed with great precision and care. Concentrating on details will bear fruit later.

Work on the circle is begun at the walk, which makes it easier for the rider to maintain the correct seat and apply the necessary aids. The teacher reminds the pupil to remain on the same track and not to allow his horse to deviate from it. As it is difficult to maintain impulsion at the walk, it may happen that the horse begins to drag his feet. In this case work on the circle should be interrupted and the horse taken two or three times around the arena at a rising trot before a correct circle at the walk is tried again. When the rider is able to ride a correct circle at the walk, which should be possible after two or three lessons, work at the trot, which is the backbone of training, may begin. As the trot is more difficult to sit, especially on a horse that is not sufficiently supple, the working trot is practiced until the pupil has no more difficulties in maintaining his seat which might influence the balance of his horse. Increasing the speed to the ordinary trot, later even to a few steps at the extended trot, will follow with the progress in maintaining the correct seat.

On the circle the pupil will best learn how to guide his horse and how to obtain the correct contact with the bit as well as the position of head and neck. Keeping a regular tempo is easier on the circle, too. He must feel the difference between the working trot and the ordinary trot and be able to demand this difference of speed from his horse. When passing from the ordinary trot into the working tempo the pushing aid of the legs is decreased and short actions given with the reins. The rein action should not degenerate into a steady pull which would induce the horse to lie on the rein but should consist of several short actions, giving and taking (the so-called half halts), while the rider sits upright and with a braced back. For the transition from the working trot into the ordinary tempo the legs are a little more firmly applied, tapping the horse's side two or three times if necessary to make him go forward. The reins are slightly given to allow the horse to take a longer stride. On a school horse it should not be necessary to give the reins too much in these transitions or even slacken them as the horse would lose the contact with the bit and consequently the regularity of the movement. It is important at this stage of training that all transitions be performed by the horse taking a steady contact on the bit. Frequent changes of speed keep the horse's attention awake and teach him to respond to even slight aids and concentrate on his rider. Moreover, his suppleness and agility are increased and contact, impulsion, and obedience improved.

Again the teacher should adapt his lesson to the requirements of the individual: horses that have a tendency to become hasty—either from zeal or from nervousness—should be worked in longer periods at the same speed to calm them down, while lazy or dull horses must be made lively by frequent changes of speed. However, the teacher is warned against practicing changes of speed too often without interspersing longer periods at the same tempo. The horse would soon try to anticipate the rider's aids and lose the faculty of maintaining a regular tempo.

The correct contact, too, is more easily obtained on the circle. Contact is closely related to the position of head and neck which is correct when the horse takes a quiet contact on the bit and moves well forward and with impulsion while carrying the rider willingly. A pupil with little experience should ride his horse with a low head and neck stretched, and not overbend him or compress him in the neck. The low position of head and neck allows the horse to arch his back and carry his rider with ease. When arching his back the horse uses his hind legs energetically and elastically and the rider is able to sit comfortably as he maintains his balance in the saddle. The rider must never try to raise his horse's head and neck unnaturally, that is, take his head up with the reins. This is especially harmful to young horses with a weak back. Raising head and neck prematurely or unnaturally renders work difficult even for horses with good conformation. It prevents the hind legs from stepping under the body and takes away impulsion and destroys the paces. Any position is bad that is obtained at the cost of the paces.

The instructor explains the meaning of correct contact which the pupil should try to obtain from his horse. It will take some time to reach this goal, and the smallest progress should be rewarded. Contact is best explained when the rider applies both reins evenly and the teacher calls his attention to the reaction of the horse, which may take a stronger contact on one side of the bit and a lighter or no contact on the other. In other words, he is stiff on one side and hollow on the other. On the stiff side the rider feels the rein like a weight, while he has nothing in his other hand. If the rider tolerated this uneven contact, the horse would seek support on the rider's hand on the stiff side (lie on the rein) while on the other side he would bend his neck to a greater degree than the body, making himself hollow. With such uneven contact on the bit the horse cannot move in balance. When asked to turn or to go on the circle to the hollow side, the horse performs the exercise incorrectly, increasing the flexion in the neck and swinging his hind quarters to the outside.

This bad habit is a serious impediment to training and

must be constantly fought. The rider applies the rein on the hollow side and tries by short giving and taking actions with the rein—half halts—on the stiff side to straighten the horse's neck. To begin with the rider may practice this aid and try to make his horse understand at a standstill. Later, however, these half halts have to be administered when in motion while the leg aids maintain the impulsion. The horse should not become slower in his movement. When the half halts have obtained the desired result and the horse takes an even contact on both reins, these unilateral rein aids must cease and should be repeated only when the horse makes himself stiff again or hollow on the other side. It is easier to turn the horse to the stiff side on which he takes contact on the bit than to the hollow side on which he bends his neck instead of turning. Therefore, in the beginning the teacher should ask his pupil to ride the circle to the stiff side. Here he will have less difficulty in executing the half halts and can ride the circle correctly and truly round.

There are two things the teacher should remember: work on the circle is only a means to teach the horse correct turns and flexion as well as an increased action of the hind legs. Secondly, when performed correctly, work on the circle is a great strain on the horse, especially on his inside hind leg which is made to bend more than the outside one. Therefore, it should not be practiced for too long at a time and should be interrupted by changing the rein or taking the horse straight along the wall. When alternating work on the circle and riding straight lines, the horse should maintain an even tempo which is demanded by his rider. This is proof that the pupil has made progress. When passing onto the circle from the straight line the horse should not become slower or increase speed when going large from the circle. This is very important as this fault is frequent with young horses and riders and may become a bad habit if not eradicated at the outset.

Besides alternating work on the circle and on straight lines the teacher must demand frequent changes of rein in order to develop both sides of the horse evenly, and should not allow his pupil—out of carelessness or laziness—to work on the same rein for too long. In this stage of training the change of rein is executed over the diagonal. The pupil takes his horse from one long side to the opposite side of the school starting about six steps after having passed the corner after the short side. The teacher insists that the pupil ride a straight line and not allow his horse to sway. As every movement should be executed with great precision, the change through the diagonal is first practiced at the walk. When performed at a rising trot later, the pupil has to change the leg he rides on, either in the center or before reaching the opposite wall. He remains in the saddle for one step and begins to rise again when the other pair of legs leaves the ground. When changing the rein the whip is changed to the other side. And the position of the horse's head is changed, too. Either in the center of the diagonal or when arriving on the long side of the school, the position of the horse's head must be adjusted to the new direction. That is, the aids are reversed and what was the inside rein becomes the outside rein. When changing the whip, for instance from the left to the right, the point of the whip is brought up by turning the left wrist and the right hand is placed above the left so that the thumb is alongside the little finger of the left hand and the point of the whip is then brought over the horse's head with the right hand. The change of the whip must never influence the contact and the position of the head which are of greater importance. Therefore, the pupil may be allowed to change the whip at a later moment.

When the young rider is able to control his horse at the walk and trot, he may begin to canter. It is much better to wait with the canter until the rider's seat is sufficiently firm than to have the rider lose his seat and disturb the horse's movement. It is the ordinary canter that is practiced at this stage of training. Work at the canter begins on the circle and from the trot as this transition is easier for horse and rider. The pupil uses both his legs, the inside leg on the girth and the outside one slightly behind the girth. Shifting his weight onto the inside seat bone, he pushes the horse forward at the trot until he passes into the canter. The lateral bend the horse must adopt on the circle and in the corners of the school will help him to strike off into the canter. If the horse does not understand immediately, the pupil may tap his whip lightly on the girth or on the inside shoulder of the horse and give a click of the tongue. From the beginning the horse should learn to strike off quietly and not rush off, as it is important for later work that he does not alter speed when passing from the trot into the canter. In the same way the canter comes to an end by a transition into the trot. Both transitions should be smooth and fluent, which results from repeated practice of this exercise. Should the unskilled rider cause the horse to strike off on the wrong lead, the teacher orders him calmly to take him into the trot again and try the strike-off once more. If the following attempts fail or, because of an incorrect seat, the horse is made to strike off into a disunited canter, it is proof that the pupil is not yet ready for the canter and the teacher must go back to the basic training and teach a correct seat. The disunited canter is a faulty pace in which the horse canters on the left lead, for instance, with the front legs and with the hind legs on the right lead.

Again it should not be forgotten to change the rein frequently. At this stage of training the pupil takes his horse into a trot, begins the circle on the other rein, and then strikes off on the other lead. After having practiced the canter on the circle until horse and rider have no more difficulty, the pupil can take his horse on a straight line. Also, beginning on the circle, the speed may be gradually reduced to the working tempo. When the strike-off on the circle presents no more problem and always comes about on the true leg, it may be practiced in the corners of the school first and on a straight line later. When there are setbacks it is best to go back on the circle and again demand the correct strike-off.

Correct halts should be practiced in this stage of training from the walk first and then from the trot, as should the move-off in both paces. The horse is brought to a halt by repeated half halts with both reins. If the horse is stiff on one side, the half halts on this side prevail over those on the hollow side. On no account should the young rider give a steady pull on the horse's mouth. It is important that at the same time the legs should be firmly applied to the horse's sides to prevent him from losing collection and coming on his forehand. When moving off, the pupil gives the reins just a little—he should not let go of them altogether—and increases the pressure of his legs.

Another exercise at this phase would be to ask the pupil to ride up to a determined point of the arena or to his teacher, which is of greater benefit than riding all sorts of figures when performed incorrectly for lack of skill.

The progressive training which has been explained in this chapter and which extends over weeks and months is at the same time a pattern for the individual lesson in the course of which all phases of training should be passed through. With the increased abilities of horse and rider, the work of the past weeks and months can be condensed into a single lesson.

Whenever difficulties occur the teacher must first find the cause in order to be able to help his pupil and give clear and comprehensive orders. He should never give stereotype commands or long-winded explanations which cannot be absorbed by the pupil on horseback. Nor must he shout at the rider. The best remedy is always to return to the basis of

1. The psychological approach to understanding the horse was due to Pluvinel

2. My great teacher and loyal partner Oberbereiter Gottlieb Polak on Siglavy, Andalusia, 1920

3. *My four-legged teacher Nero after his victory at the European Championship in Budapest, 1935*

4. *Work on the longe*

5. *Running reins*

6. *Snaffle*

7. *Double bridle*

8. Walk on the loose rein should be the beginning and the end of every riding lesson

9. The impulsive trot is the backbone of training

training: if the horse is reluctant to go forward and loses impulsion, he should be taken forward at a brisk rising trot. If he comes behind or above the bit he must again be taught to seek contact with a low head and a long neck.

For better understanding, here is an outline for the program of a training session in this stage. This is by no means a rigid pattern of work but is meant to give the instructor ideas and suggestions for planning his daily lesson.

It should always begin with walk on the long, preferably loose, rein to give horse and rider the opportunity to become familiar with the place. After hours spent in the stables the horse will have time to stretch and adapt himself to carrying a rider. The duration of this period of walk depends on the age, the temperament, and the degree of training of the horse. Young and frisky horses with little training may be given up to ten minutes of a quiet walk with long rhythmic strides. For older or lazy ones, five minutes will be sufficient. In another five minutes they are made lively by a brisk rising trot which builds up the necessary impulsion.

During the following ten minutes the horse should be warmed up and relaxed, which is best achieved by trotting him with short loose steps with the reins as long as possible. According to his degree of training, riding large circles, serpentines, and various turns with changes of rein increases his attention and suppleness, especially when the rider succeeds in obtaining these exercises mainly by the aids of weight (shifting his weight to the side of the change of direction). The sequence of steps must not be accelerated or slowed down or the horse allowed to drop into a walk. If he increases the speed, which occurs frequently with nervous or spirited horses or with young ones as yet unable to maintain their balance in this loosening trot, the rider practices transitions into the walk brought about by half halts with very long reins and then quietly breaks into the short trot again. If during this loosening work the horse drops into a walk, trying to avoid the strain of these short steps at the trot, riding him around the arena at the ordinary rising trot will give him new impulsion. In most cases the object of this work will be reached: the horse is relaxed and his muscles and sinews loosened up and he concentrates on his rider.

Now regular work at the trot, which is the basis of all training, may begin. Depending on the degree of progress, the working tempo or the collected trot (with more advanced horses) alternates with the ordinary sitting trot while the rider concentrates on maintaining the correct contact as well as the impulsion. Work on the large circle and on the straight line, riding correct corners, and the precise performance of turns and small circles develop the horse's obedience and suppleness, reflected by a better carriage and form of the horse as well as the correct seat of the rider. It goes without saying that the teacher does not take his eyes off his pupil and continuously administers advice and correction.

As already mentioned, the duration of warming up and the initial work at the trot depend on the degree of the training. With some horses, those that are older, advanced in training, or intelligent and with good temperament, a shorter lapse of time may suffice and regular work may begin after twenty minutes. Others with little training or with a nervous and difficult temperament need more time to supple up until they find their mental and physical balance. This is also true for work after a day of rest. Here, it seems necessary to emphasize that work after several days of rest must never be overdone but should be built up progressively. If this rule is not observed, the consequence might be azoturia, which is commonly called Monday morning sickness. This sickness generally leads to severe damage of the horse's health and more often than not to his death. This consideration for the horse's health during warming up as well as during the training, even if it means momentarily renouncing any further progress, is never a waste of time but helps to consolidate the foundations of training: suppleness, impulsion, and obedience. For obvious reasons, then, this example of a lesson must on no account be followed to the letter but must be adapted to the individual case.

After these thirty minutes the lesson continues with the exercises that horse and rider have learned already or are to learn. We have seen repeatedly that the emphasis is on *how* the horse performs a certain exercise and not on *what* he shows. Now the rider practices the correct strike-off into the canter from the trot, at first on the circle, later in the corners of the riding school, and finally on the straight line. Next comes work at the canter with changes of speed (ordinary canter, working, and collected canter) while special care is taken that the horse remains straight. Periods of walk with the reins applied are interspersed, as are halts and moving off into the walk or trot while observing the correct position of the horse's head and the accurate application of the aids. Rider and teacher must not be carried away, however, by their zeal and forget short breaks between the various periods of work, which depend on the strength and the degree of training of both horse and rider and should always consist of a walk on the loose rein. When given after a well-performed exercise, it is a reward for both and a stimulation for further work.

For pupils who are in training for dressage classes, the teacher may choose a test from the book of dressage programs issued by all National Federations and ranging from first level to difficult classes. They rarely exceed the duration of six to twelve minutes and should be ridden to command. The teacher must not, however, drill his pupil by repeating the test over and over again, which would lead to mechanization and is therefore to be avoided by all means. Riding a test helps to detect weak spots in the rider's or the horse's schooling which may be eliminated once the cause has been ascertained.

An experienced and conscientious riding instructor prepares the lesson by planning a program of work adapted to the abilities of his pupil and which he follows step by step in the course of the lesson. He must, however, not cling obstinately to the chosen program, for it is above all the correctness of the exercises that matters. Therefore, he might be forced to abbreviate or change his program and concentrate on detecting the cause of some fault and eliminating it. If the teacher takes the trouble to make short notes on each lesson, jotting down remarks, observations, and suggestions, he builds a file he will find extremely helpful in case of setbacks or faults which reoccur or when the student returns to the lesson after an interval of time. He should encourage his pupil, too, to keep a diary to which he may resort when working on his own at any later period. The distant beginnings of the present book as well as of my previous publications were the notes I made on my lessons when I was teaching young officers at the Austrian Cavalry School.

The teacher should avoid exceeding the duration of forty-five minutes to one hour for a lesson, as fatigue of horse or rider would have a negative influence on the training. There is a deep meaning in the sentence which the riding instructor as well as any rider working his own horse should forever remember: I have time. On the other hand, this axiom must not be misused to disguise laziness and lack of system.

The majority of pupils will have reached the goal of their ambition when they are able to take their horse into the desired direction and work him even without the teacher and maintain his form. This methodical and logical instruction provides the beginner with a sound foundation which may serve as a starting point for further development either in dressage or in jumping. Depending on the skill and the talent of the pupil and the quality of the school horse, this may take a number of weeks up to several months. In some cases it may take half a year or even longer. The teacher should again be reminded that patience is the cornerstone of instruction and that he can never obtain satisfactory results by forcing a pupil but only by progressing conscientiously step by step.

It is the best proof of a good lesson when time seems to become too short for both teacher and pupil. If the lesson seemed endless to one of them or even to both, the verdict is that the instruction was bad.

B. ON A LONGE HORSE OR ON THE PUPIL'S OWN HORSE

Nowadays there is very rarely a well-trained school horse at the instructor's disposal on which to continue the lessons after the training on the longe has been completed. Nor can every ambitious rider afford a trained dressage horse. He may be able, however, to buy a young horse for whose training he has not yet acquired the necessary knowledge. Teacher and pupil, consequently, may face two possibilities in continuing their work: either the young rider provides his own untrained horse and instruction is given to both at the same time, or the lessons continue on the horse that has served as the longe horse.

A longe horse is not a special breed but one of those unfortunate creatures to be found in most riding schools. Nature has denied them good conformation or talent and they were never allowed to rise above the lowest standards. Sadder still, they might have seen better times in their lives and, because of age or sickness, have to earn their oats as longe horses. In some respects they are the ideal mounts for a beginner as they are calm and good-natured, not inclined to fits of temperament or gaiety, but, rather, intent on making life as easy for themselves as possible.

It is the better solution when the teacher continues the lessons on the same horse on which he longed his pupil. During the last part of the longeing lessons the pupil has learned to use the rein and leg aids when riding on the circle. Now he can begin to go around the arena along the wall at a walk, trying to influence his horse with reins and legs as he has learned to do on the circle.

If the teacher uses a longe horse that he does not know, it is advisable to longe his pupil for three to four days as he teaches him the correct guidance. During this transitional period horse and rider may become familiar with each other while the instructor observes the horse and is able to interfere immediately with longe and whip in case of difficulties.

In both cases the teacher passes in the same manner from work on the longe to work in the whole arena. He should remember, however, that a horse used to moving on a circle for a longer period of time will have difficulty going on straight lines, especially when he is alone in the arena with no other horse to follow as he would have in a group. While still on the longe, the correct length of the stirrups is adjusted and the teacher takes the horse several times around the circle, which should be as large as possible. At the point where the circle touches the wall of the arena, he asks the pupil to take the horse straight along the wall for two to four meters, pushing him with longe and whip if necessary. As the next step he shortens the longe to about two meters, walking at the horse's shoulder, and asks the pupil to ride at a walk along the wall around the arena. Thus he is prepared to interfere before major difficulties arise: with the longe if the horse accelerates or comes out of control, or by showing the whip when he begins to drag his feet or try to edge away from the wall. A longe horse should be accustomed to this kind of aid and accept it willingly. Having practiced the walk in this manner on both reins, the teacher lengthens the longe until he no longer walks beside the horse but behind him. With the teacher disappearing from his range of vision, the horse has to concentrate on the rider. Nevertheless, the instructor is immediately at hand in case of difficulties with which the young rider is unable to cope.

When the longe is dispensed with, the instruction continues step by step in the same manner as explained on pages 68ff about the school horse. It is obvious that progress will come more slowly as faults and habits need to be eradicated in the horse and he must be improved in many respects. His contact with the bit should not present any special problems provided that he was longed correctly and with side reins. If, because of the unskilled hands of the pupil, the contact becomes unsteady and, particularly if the horse throws his head up, side reins should be used during the first weeks of instruction. They should not, however, be adjusted so tightly as to compress the horse's neck but allow him the correct position of head and neck while taking a light contact. The more serious problem is impulsion, which the horse is probably lacking after having gone on the longe for a longer period of time. Therefore, the horse must be ridden forward at a brisk speed and at the rising trot until he shows forward urge without being pushed. From this moment on it is possible to begin various exercises.

It will take more time to obtain the gradual collection and the position of the head, and it may often be necessary for the teacher to mount and to correct. On the other hand, when riding the horse himself at intervals, the instructor finds new ways and ideas as to how best to advise his pupil and help to overcome his problems. It is understood that the teacher demands only those exercises the horse is able to perform. The recommended exercises are enumerated in Chapter 10A. Although any riding horse should be able to execute these exercises, they might represent difficulties for an ancient longe horse with which the beginner cannot cope on his own. Again it may be necessary for the teacher to mount the horse, which is preferable to all sorts of long-winded explanations the pupil is as yet unable to put into practice. Various shortcomings are likely to appear with so imperfect a school horse and have to be dealt with by the teacher. He should ride the horse first and prepare him for the different exercises which he then demands from the student. Above all, he must teach the horse to go forward and with impulsion as the pupil's influence is still too weak and in trying to push the horse forward he would spoil his seat. It may also be necessary for the teacher to ride the horse repeatedly to eliminate faults the pupil may have caused. These problems slow down the progress of the pupil and his training will take much longer compared with instruction on a school horse.

Similar, if much more difficult, is the situation the teacher faces when he has brought the training on the longe to an end and begins instruction on the pupil's own horse which has had little training so far. There are many positive sides to the pupil riding his own horse, in whom he certainly has much more personal interest and to whom he is more attached than to a rented horse. On the other hand, instruction is made more difficult by the fact that the horse himself is still untrained. The teacher deals with two pupils at the same time and must adjust his demands to the abilities of both and synchronize the procedures. It is an interesting and rewarding task to educate two creatures, bring them along, and make them become friends. It is certainly a difficult task, too, which demands great knowledge and experience together with physical proficiency. Here more than in the previous cases, instruction is not given by words alone. On the contrary, the teacher must ride the horse frequently and at regular intervals, especially when beginning a new phase of training or when the pupil finds himself in a deadlock. The lesson must progress according to the abilities of the horse, and, again, the teacher must remember not to demand any exercises the horse is as yet unable to perform. Besides, both teacher and pupil must be prepared for a long period of training with little visible progress at times.

With these facts in mind, the teacher begins by riding the pupil's horse along the wall of the school at a lively walk on the loose rein. He demands mainly that the horse remains straight along the wall, does not sway, and moves well forward without being constantly pushed. The horse should stretch his neck and carry his head low, which makes him arch his back and carry the rider's weight more easily. If he shies from any objects, specks of light, etc., and does not pay attention to the rider, he should be allowed to take a look at these objects. The teacher leads him up to them, talking to him and rewarding him with sugar when he approaches. Even if it has to be repeated several times, this method is the surest way to success and much better than even the slightest punishment.

When the horse moves calmly along the wall at a good walk on both reins, the teacher rides him briskly forward at the rising trot to build up the necessary impulsion. At the trot the horse will probably shy away from the very same objects because they come much faster into the field of his vision. Again punishment is of no help; the rider should take his horse into a walk or bring him to a halt, again quietly show him the object of his fear, and try to pass once more at the trot. Made familiar with the frightening objects in this way, the horse will soon concentrate on his rider and not look around for distraction. The horse should go equally well on both reins at the walk and the trot, execute the change of rein over the diagonal at the walk, and perform willingly the transition from the walk into the trot and vice versa before the teacher allows the pupil to mount and execute the same exercises.

To begin with, the pupil's seat, which he has learned on the longe, must be controlled. He should be constantly reminded that he must not hold on to the reins or grip the horse with his legs. After correct training on the longe the horse should be accustomed to going at the walk with a long neck and an arched back and maintain this posture also at the trot. It is the fault of the unskilled pupil if the horse loses his position. When his lack of routine makes the horse raise his head and come off the bit at the trot, consequently dropping his back, side reins should be used for the time being in order to maintain the position of head and neck which the young horse has been taught on the longe. He must not be allowed to adopt the habit of going with a raised head and a dropped back. Such a position would spoil progress made so far and misdirect any further training. Under no circumstances should the teacher give running reins into the hands of his pupil, as unfortunately happens quite often, in order to force the horse into the desired position of head and neck by the lever action on the bit. With the ends of the running rein clasped into the girth and the reins running through the rings of the snaffle into the hands of the rider, the slightest action of the rein works with double effect on the horse's mouth. The use of the running rein is of very doubtful utility and is criticized with justification even with an accomplished rider, but in the hands of a student it is a crime.

When the pupil begins to ride without the longe but his pushing aids are not yet effective enough, the teacher must, besides watching his seat, warn him against tapping his legs constantly against the horse's flanks. He would not only lose the correct grip of his knees but above all blunt the horse's sensitiveness to the leg aids. So far the rider's leg aids and the forward movement of the horse (never forget that the horse must learn, too!) were supported by the instructor's whip. In this stage the pupil begins to replace the teacher's aids by applying the riding whip or tapping it lightly on the horse's shoulder. Later the whip is used on the girth just behind the rider's leg. As already mentioned, the rider must be extremely careful when using the whip not to jerk at the horse's mouth at the same time, which is even more harmful to the horse than when the pupil holds on to the reins to restore his balance. How should the horse understand the pushing aid of the whip if a simultaneous jerk at the rein prevents him from going forward?

To begin with, the daily work is done on long straight lines at the walk and trot, alternating short periods at the trot with equal or even longer periods of walk on the loose rein. These periods of walk help to avoid tiring the young horse and making him lose the vivacity of his paces. The pupil, too, rests in these periods of walk and readjusts his seat in the saddle. For the teacher they represent the best opportunity to correct the student's seat and hands and explain the following exercises. Moreover, in this way the pupil learns to execute the transition from the trot into the walk and vice versa which belongs to the basic exercises for all kinds of riding. In these periods of walk the horse must not be allowed to move sluggishly, dragging his feet, but by the pushing aids should be encouraged to a regular long stride.

The teacher must have a thorough knowledge of the character, the mental and physical abilities of both his pupils and build up the instruction accordingly, increasing his demands step by step. The lessons adjusted to the individual will win in no time over a stereotype way of training. Weak horses that tire easily—which may be concluded from the way they begin to drag their feet and forge into the front hoofs—should be worked in shorter periods and strong, frisky ones for a longer time. The duration of the periods of work depends also on the age, skill, and stamina of the pupil whose fatigue would be the cause of faults in seat and guidance.

For the necessary impulsion and forward urge, the rising trot is practiced. The teacher has already taught the horse in this exercise and must now teach the pupil the principles described on pages 56 and 73-74. It is important that the pupil not disturb the horse's balance by unnatural movements of his upper part which are not in concordance with the motion of the horse. As a remedy he should sit through several steps in between the rising trot, especially when passing the corners of the school. This conveys to him the feeling for the rhythm of the movement. When riding at the rising trot he must not heave himself from the saddle but allow himself to be lifted up lightly by the movement of the horse. He will then have no problem knowing the leg he rides on. When the pupil practices these few steps at the sitting trot, the teacher should see that the horse does not slacken the speed, which would be a warning of his lack of forward urge. Neither should he increase the speed when the rider passes from the sitting trot into the rising trot, because this is a sure sign that it is not the rider who commands his horse but the horse that follows his own will.

In this phase of training of horse and rider, the reins should be as long as possible without, however, losing contact with the bit. The instructor must impress upon the pupil that a long rein is not a loose rein. If the rider misinterprets the expression "long rein" and allows his horse to perform the exercises without contact, he will harm not only his young horse's sinews and muscles but also his whole carriage, as well as his mental and physical development.

For the time being the teacher asks the rider to pass through the corners on a large arc or circle and with unilateral rein aids, that is, with only the inside rein without applying the outside rein. The rider's weight is shifted on the inside seat bone. When the correct contact has been understood by both horse and rider as the training progresses, the pupil may begin to learn how to take his horse through the corners according to the classical rules.

The halt is first practiced from the walk. It is important that the horse stand quietly and on all four legs waiting for further commands of his rider. With young horses the halt should be of short duration which is gradually increased. It is easier for the horse to carry the rider's weight in movement than at the standstill. It is a good exercise gradually to extend the duration of the correct halt just before dismounting because the horse will accept the end of work and dismounting as a reward.

Up to this moment, mainly the rising trot was practiced and the horse made to go forward with impulsion. Now the sitting trot will take a larger part of the lesson. At first it should be practiced on the circle. Although the horse had been made familiar with the circle during the training on the longe after going on straight lines for some time, he should again be accustomed to the circle at the walk. The teacher insists that the tempo remain unaltered and the circle truly round. The function of longe and whip must be replaced by the pupil's leg and rein aids. The same is demanded at the trot. The horse is made familiar with the sitting trot by alternating the sitting and the rising trot on the circle. Later the same exercise is practiced along the wall.

When the horse performs walk and trot willingly and does not get excited in the transitions, the pupil may try the canter, on the circle at first as explained on pages 82–84. It is important that the young horse not get out of control and become conscious of his strength because the young rider could not cope with the situation. It is understood that the instructor introduces the horse to the canter before allowing the pupil to mount and try to canter.

At this stage of training, horse and rider should be ready

to be gradually introduced to going on outdoor rides as explained in the following section.

11. Cross-country riding and jumping

Riding cross-country and over obstacles belongs to the program of training of every rider. For the sake of clarity I have made it the subject of a separate chapter. It is also a vital part of the schooling of every riding horse. For a horse that has been trained for dressage or jumping but that may not be used for going out cross-country because of his temperament or other difficulties reveals a fundamental and unforgivable deficiency in his basic training. The correct and systematic work in the riding school, however, is the best preparation for riding cross-country. Riding out, in turn, increases impulsion and has a stimulating effect on the instruction in the arena. During the three to six months of training as described on page 84, the teacher should seek the opportunity to take his pupils out either in a group or singly. This constitutes recreation for the horse, increases his forward urge, and makes him familiar with different surroundings and various noises and objects. For the pupil it means physical and mental relaxation, and both horse and rider will accept it as a reward.

The experienced teacher will not change abruptly from working in a confined space to riding in the open and from moving on flat even ground to going over rough terrain but will proceed carefully with gradual increase of difficulties and thus possibly spare his pupil any unpleasant surprises. Therefore, he does not take the pupil out before he is able to guide his horse without the teacher's assistance on straight lines and in turns, bring him to a halt, and move on again. He should also be able to ride the rising trot. The teacher must explain to his pupil that when riding cross-country only the rising trot is practiced and never the sitting trot, especially on roads or hard ground. However, in the transition from the walk into the trot and vice versa, the first and last few steps of the trot are ridden at the sitting trot, which permits the rider better control over his horse. During the ride the instructor reminds his pupil at intervals that when trotting for a longer duration of time the rider must change the leg he rides on exactly as when changing the rein in the arena. At the rising trot the rider's weight is supported by one and the same hind leg every other step while there is no weight on the other leg. The change of leg is important to avoid wearing out the horse's hind legs.

For the first excursions the teacher chooses quiet roads and paths so that the horse will not get excited and the pupil will have an opportunity to study his horse's behavior outside the riding hall. For the same reason he begins at the walk and continues at it for some time to make sure that his pupil maintains his correct seat and does not hold on to the reins any tighter than when in the ring. When the horse remains calm, a short period at the rising trot may follow, but not in the direction of the stables, for then the horse will be more difficult to control. Should he begin to hurry or even try to run away, which might happen after weeks of work in the indoor school, he must be taken into the walk immediately and horse and rider calmed down. The pupil should not become afraid that he may lose control over his horse. Nervousness should be avoided as it would be transmitted to the horse. The walk is the best pace to calm and control the horse, who should never become aware of how easily he may evade his rider's guidance by rushing off or jumping aside. Such unpleasant surprises, which might entail numerous difficulties, may be avoided or at least reduced to the minimum by proceeding logically and carefully. From one cross-country ride to the next, the pupil will be able to sustain longer periods at the trot and find them easier, for instruction in the school ring continues in between excursions and increases his abilities and skill.

In the beginning the teacher should be prepared to meet all sorts of unforeseen incidents. Consequently, he should bring a leading rein to be able to lead the pupil's horse in case of severe difficulties. It is particularly helpful when riding out with a single pupil. The leading rein is made of the same material as the longe and is one and a half meters long with a loop for the teacher's hand on one end and a clasp or a buckle on the other which is fastened into the snaffle of the pupil's horse. This precaution should not be regarded as exaggerated anxiety but as another means to convey to the pupil the feeling of security and consolidate his confidence in the horse.

Young horses with a spooky temperament are sometimes afraid of various objects or places and try to edge away from them or refuse to advance. At the first sign of such bad behavior the teacher tells the pupil to push his horse forward at the sitting trot and even take his upper part back behind the vertical, which allows him to sit more firmly in the saddle and apply the pushing aids with better effect. If the young rider is unable to succeed, the teacher passes in front and appeals to the herding instinct of the pupil's horse, who is made to follow closely. At first, the horse should be given the opportunity to take a look at the object of his fear while the rider pats him and calms him and tries to win his confidence again. If repeated attempts fail, the teacher must on no account be carried away and drive the pupil's horse forward with his riding whip. He might cause a fight which the young rider cannot carry through and in which he is unable to help him. Rather he should cautiously grasp the excited horse's bridle and lead him on, riding at his side. This is a case when the leading rein should be at hand. At any rate, such an incident is proof that the horse is not yet sufficiently reliable for cross-country rides. His obedience and his confidence in his rider must be improved by work in the arena, practicing exercises such as halts and move-on, changes of pace and speed, riding of turns and large circles.

Special care must be taken when a beginner is taken out on his young and still rather green horse. Here it is most important that the rider has learned to maintain an independent seat. Before going out for the first time the pupil should lead his horse out of the stables and up and down in front of the riding school and repeat this exercise several times to make the horse used to different surroundings. The first outdoor rides should follow a short lesson in the arena in which the horse has worked off his friskiness and they should be done mainly at the walk. If the beginner rides in a group, the others must by all means be considerate and adjust to his abilities until he and his horse have grown accustomed to riding out. On the other hand, the herding instinct helps the young rider to guide his horse.

When several rides with periods of various duration at the walk and trot have been undertaken without difficulties and horse and rider have become familiar with the terrain, the teacher may intersperse a short period at the canter. Preferably he chooses an even terrain not in the direction of the stables, for the reasons explained above, and begins to canter after the horses have gone for several periods at the walk and trot. The teacher strikes off from the trot and brings the canter to an end before the horses, stimulated by the brisk pace, begin to rush. After the canter the horses should be rewarded with a period at the walk, if possible on the long rein.

There is a bad habit which the teacher should bring to the pupil's attention. When outdoors the horse constantly tries to eat grass, leaves, or twigs and the rider should try to prevent this. As with life in general, so with riding: while at work the attention must be centered on what one is doing. While under the saddle the horse must concentrate on his rider. This does not mean, however, that the horse should not be allowed to graze when the rider dismounts for a rest at a pleasant spot.

These excursions are meant as a recreation and a reward for the rider and even more so for the horse. Consequently, for the sake of our four-legged partner the trot should be avoided and the canter never ridden on rocky ground. The pupil is too busy with the problems of seat and guidance to be able to pay attention to the footing. It is the teacher's responsibility to spare the horse unnecessary strain.

The present phase of instruction comprises also the initial training for jumping. It is certainly not a special preparation for show jumping, about which many books have been written. Here it is a question of teaching the beginner to take low and medium obstacles which may be encountered on cross-country rides. Although an old joke says that there is no fence so high or so wide that a rider could not circle around it, jumping easy obstacles does certainly belong to the schooling of every rider. Almost any serious cross-country course presents various obstacles and should not be undertaken before the rider knows how to jump. Even with dressage classes, a jump over a medium fence is demanded as a test of the horse's obedience and his usefulness as a riding horse.

When the pupil has acquired a firm seat in the saddle, he learns how to jump in a systematic procedure preferably at the end of the daily lesson. The horse has worked off his friskiness and, besides, may be sent into the stables as a reward for a well-performed jump. The rider takes him at first at a walk and later at the trot over a bar of wood placed on the ground. This makes the horse familiar with the unaccustomed object on the ground. If necessary he should be led up to the bar and allowed to take a look at it. The pupil should gradually get used to a more abrupt movement of the horse. It may happen that the first time the horse jumps unnecessarily high over the bar. In this case the teacher should warn the rider not to fall back with his upper body or hold on to the reins and jerk the horse in the mouth. On the contrary, he must try by leaning slightly forward and gripping firmly with his knees to maintain his balance in this unaccustomed movement of his horse. If he does not succeed, it is better to hold on to the pommel of the saddle than to hang on the reins and disturb the horse.

The horse must learn to maintain the sequence of steps of the walk or the trot even when going over an object on the ground and for this he needs his physical and mental balance. When horse and rider maintain their balance, the bar is placed on props about a foot above the ground. Most riding schools provide cavalletti (a bar fixed between two x-shaped supports) which may be used at different heights according to their position. For more difficult jumps, two or more cavalletti may be placed one on top of the other. Now the pupil takes his horse over the cavalletti at the trot. In the beginning the horse may try to rush or strike off into the canter or begin to sway. He should be calmed down and the exercise repeated until he trots over the bar without losing the rhythm and just by lifting his legs a little higher, not touching the bar. Then the same exercise may be performed at the canter. The horse should not begin to rush or go out of control, which would make it difficult for the rider to maintain his seat. The best way to combat this habit of storming a fence is to take the horse into a lower pace, that is, from the canter into the trot or from the trot into the walk. After a few steps the pupil continues to ride up to the fence as before, either at the canter or at the trot.

During these jumping exercises, which should not, however, be exaggerated, the teacher must constantly control the pupil's seat. He should lean slightly forward, sitting with a low heel and a firm knee regardless of whether his horse trots, canters, or jumps over the fence. The reins should be somewhat lengthened without losing contact with the horse's mouth. When watching the horse the teacher may judge the pupil's seat: if the pupil loses his balance or disturbs the house's mouth or back, the horse will become nervous or even violent. Therefore, the height of the fence must not be increased until the teacher has eliminated these faults. During the daily lesson he concentrates on the pupil's seat and lightness of hands. Instruction in riding and jumping must complement each other.

When the pupil can take the cavalletti in correct manner, he may begin to jump higher and, more important, different obstacles, that is, different in height and width as well as in form and color. These might include simple fences not higher than two-feet-four to three-feet-four of natural bars, wooden boards, or brush fences, as well as double fences of equally modest dimensions, such as oxers, etc. Dimensions are less important than the varied forms and colors to which the horse should grow accustomed and so lose his spookiness when out in the field.

If, even in a more advanced stage, the horse continues to become violent when asked to jump in these practice sessions, the rider should turn him away from the obstacle at about ten meters' distance and repeat this maneuver several times. This procedure calms the horse down and prevents him from accelerating his speed when going toward the fence. However, he should not be ridden too closely up to the obstacle and then turned away, as this would make too great a demand on his obedience. On one hand, it undermines his willingness to jump and on the other, being turned aside just before the fence might induce him to break away from it at another moment. When the pupil has mastered these problems in the arena the teacher may send him out with a clear conscience.

In order to prevent misunderstandings I want to underline that there is a fundamental difference between outdoor excursions on horseback, with which we have dealt so far and which take the rider mainly over roads, paths, and fields, and real cross-country rides which lead up and down hill over rough terrain and natural obstacles and at a much faster speed. A cross-country ride demands much more knowledge and ability from the rider as well as from the horse than a mere outing. It is mainly practiced in groups—Three- and One-day Events excepted—and may reach an ultimate in hunting to hounds. Hunts on horseback after the stag, the boar, or the fox tracked by a pack of hounds demands wide-open countryside which is rarely to be found in Europe. Instead, a scent is laid ahead of the group by one of the riders and is tracked by the hounds with the riders following the pack.

Again the instructor must prepare his pupils by gradual increase of demands in cross-country rides and after adequate progress in the general instruction. Then horse and rider will take pleasure in hunting. The rider shortens the stirrup leathers for two to five holes and with a low heel and a firm knee stands up in his stirrups when cantering. He leans slightly forward and takes his weight off the horse's back to make work easier for him. Only in cross-country riding is the canter ridden in this manner.

As some horses become excited when in a group, the experienced teacher rides mainly at the walk and trot for the first few outings. Horse and rider must also become gradually accustomed to uneven ground. While so far they went mainly in the arena or on bridle paths, now they learn to go over slopes uphill and at the walk at first. The group should begin to ride downhill on a more gentle slope and practice on steeper ones when all riders have their horses well under control. Regardless of the pace and whether uphill or downhill, the rider takes his upper part forward. The steeper the hill, the more forward must he lean, thus helping his horse to maintain his balance.

In the beginning, the group canters on more even ground. When there are difficulties at the first canter, the teacher must on no account risk a fight between the inexperienced pupil and his horse. A rider who fights with his horse presents not only a sorry sight but also spoils his horse's schooling. He may drive it to actions, committed out of fright or despair, with which he cannot cope. If the horse has come to detect his rider's weakness, he will, helped by his good memory, try forever to take advantage of it. In such cases the entire group must pass into the walk. The pupil tries to calm his horse until he is going on a long or even loose rein. Experience has taught us that a horse finds his mental balance better and faster when going with a long neck and a low head. He arches his back and carries his rider with more ease. Besides, in this position a horse will never be naughty but always announce any shying or bucking by first raising his head, thus warning his rider who is then able to shorten the reins in time and sit more firmly in the saddle. This is said to remind the rider never to divert his attention from his horse. While he is in the saddle he should concentrate on his partner and observe his behavior all the time. A horse feels immediately any absent-mindedness of his rider and may take advantage of it.

When the general order has been restored, a second period at the canter may be attempted. The riding teacher brings it to an end by passing into the trot or walk before the excitable horses might become violent again. This procedure teaches obedience to the horse and makes the pupil confident that he can master his mount. Only then does the teacher allow his group to canter uphill and, later, downhill.

When jumping over various obstacles such as hedges, fences, low walls, or tree trunks, the rider on the most reliable horse should head the group. Making use of the herding instinct, the other riders may jump more easily. Should the first horse refuse to jump or break away from the obstacle, however, the herding instinct would have a negative effect and induce the group to follow the bad example. Therefore, and also in case of a fall, the riders should not follow each other too closely over a fence.

Jumping over or into water demands special preparation. The shining surface is unfamiliar and frightening to most horses. On his excursions the rider usually avoids stepping into puddles primarily to save extra work for his groom. Now he must give his horse the opportunity to take a good look at the water before asking him to jump across or into it. Before jumping into a brook or a pond for the first time, he should make his horse wade into the water. If, however, the horse begins to paw in the water with his forefoot, the teacher must warn his pupil to drive his horse out immediately. After such preliminary pawing the horse usually lies down and rolls. After jumping into water the horses should never be kept standing still but should remain in motion. The teacher must impress upon his pupils that carelessness in this respect might entail serious ailments of the hoofs such as laminitis (*Pedodermatitis aseptica*).

The duration of the cross-country rides is gradually extended and the degree of difficulties increased until the rider feels completely at ease in any terrain. It is the nicest reward for the teacher when both horses and pupils enjoy the cross-country rides.

4

DRESSAGE

It is the aim of every riding instructor to further his pupil to the best of his abilities. He should, however, not be tempted by his own ambition or vanity to teach his pupil any exercises for which he is not ready. Even with a talented pupil a sound foundation is necessary. Besides, if there is no suitable school horse available, teaching exercises on a horse that is not up to the demands would lead to caricatures, as, unfortunately, may be observed quite often. An ambitious pupil does not learn much in this way and risks spoiling the young horse as well as deviating from the right path himself. Such procedure casts a doubtful light on the teacher's reputation. For, as we've seen before, it is first of all expected from a teacher that he be able to appraise the capacities of his pupil and know how much he can demand from his assistant the horse.

I repeat that it is not the object of this book to supply the riding teacher with detailed advice for the various fields of the sport of riding such as dressage, jumping, or combined

10. Canter

11. Shoulder-in

12. The horse must concentrate on his rider also at the halt

13. Half pass

14. Cross-country rides improve the horse's impulsion and give a pleasant note to instruction

15. When teaching a group the instructor concentrates by turns on every pupil

16. On a steep slope

17. Jumping simple obstacles is part of the basic training of horse and rider

18. Your horse should be your friend!

training. These subjects are too vast to be thoroughly discussed in a single book. However, basic dressage will be explained in detail, as it is the basis from which all three kinds of riding develop. (Minute instruction for schooling in advanced dressage may be found in my previous book, *The Complete Training of Horse and Rider*, while for show jumping and combined training there exist several excellent books whose authors have practiced these aspects successfully themselves.)

12. On a school horse

When the pupil is able to ride a school horse correctly at walk, trot, and canter, perform correct transitions from one pace to another, and execute precise circles and turns as well as straight lines, work at the collected paces may begin. At first it should be on the circle, on which the rider can influence and collect his horse better. Collection can be taught in movement only, never at a standstill. From the working trot the speed is gradually reduced by half halts while the legs remain firmly applied, making the horse's hind legs step well under his body. In this exercise it is of utmost importance that the reduced speed be obtained, not by slower but by shorter steps, forcing the horse to lift his legs higher off the ground. When correctly collected the horse becomes shorter in his body and the action of his legs becomes more elevated. The teacher must make his pupil understand that he should not make his horse shorter by pulling at the reins and that collection demands much impulsion. Therefore, he asks him at intervals to ride forward at a brisk ordinary trot and then make use again of the impulsion for the collected trot.

With collection a frequent fault appears which the pupil

might not feel but which must be immediately corrected by the teacher. In order to spare himself the effort of stepping under his body with the hind legs, the horse becomes crooked, that is, he swings his hind quarters away from the track and the hind feet no longer step into the hoofprints of the front feet but to the side. During the entire training the instructor must call the pupil's attention to this severe fault. The horse is straightened when in motion. It is easiest for the pupil to straighten his horse at the trot along the wall. The rider takes the forehand away from the wall with both reins until the hind legs follow the hoofprints of the front legs. Both legs push the horse forward. The action of the outside rein is most important because using the inside rein alone would induce the horse to bend his neck to the inside but not take his forehand in.

Up to this stage the corners were ridden well rounded. Now that the pupil is able to perform the collected trot on the circle and on a straight line, he learns to ride correctly through the corners. The turn in a corner correctly ridden corresponds to an arc of a circle of three steps' radius. The outside rein leads the horse into the corner while the rider pushes him forward with both legs. He sits on the inside seat bone and must not lean forward or remain behind the movement with his upper body. The inside rein leads the horse through the corner, while the outside leg behind the girth prevents the hind quarters from swinging to the outside. The inside leg on the girth maintains the motion and bends the horse in his whole body. Speed and rhythm of the trot must remain unaltered and the horse must not lose his balance.

The collected canter is taught when work at the collected trot is well established and presents no more problems. Again on the circle, the rider reduces the speed at the working canter by half halts while the leg aids maintain a lively rhythm of the canter. As with the trot, so with the canter, collection does not mean slower action but shorter and higher bounds. The collected canter represents a greater effort to the horse than the collected trot, and for this reason the teacher should be content with short periods in the beginning. Alternating periods at the working speed or the ordinary canter with the collected canter helps to restore impulsion and forward urge, making the hind legs jump well under the body. It is certainly not to be called a collected canter when, even though slowing down his speed in the sequence of steps, the horse becomes longer in his whole body and drags his hind legs. Instead of moving in a three-beat canter, he moves in four beats, which is a very severe fault. The horse's movement becomes hobbling and unpleasant, difficult to sit, and conveys to the rider a hard and uncomfortable feeling. In this case the teacher must interfere immediately and ask the pupil to increase the speed in order to regain impulsion.

In this phase of training the strike-off into the canter from the walk and the halt as well as the transitions from the canter into these paces should be taught. These exercises are of practical value for any rider in any branch of the sport. They should not, however, be attempted before the pupil is able to strike off from an even tempo at the trot without accelerating the speed and to pass from the canter again into a regular trot which must not be hasty. Both exercises should be performed on the circle and on the straight line.

For the strike-off from the walk, the same aids are employed as for the strike-off from the trot. The outside leg slightly behind the girth announces the canter and the inside leg pushing on the girth brings about the strike-off. The teacher reminds the rider to sit in this moment a little more firmly on the inside seat bone. He must also give the correct position to the horse's head with the inside rein and use it together with the inside leg to prevent the horse from bringing his hind quarters to the inside and performing a crooked strike-off. The teacher should not allow the pupil to try to obtain the strike-off by twisting his body and sliding about in the saddle, nor should he lean forward or pull at the reins or demand the strike-off with the outside leg, which would provoke a crooked strike-off. As pointed out repeatedly, in this stage of training the question is no longer that the horse strikes off into the canter but how and upon what aids he does so. Also, the teacher should insist that the horse canter straight on a single track. The horse is straightened at the canter in exactly the same way as at the trot—by taking the forehand away from the wall—but it is much more difficult to obtain a straight horse at the canter, so this bad habit must not be tolerated from the beginning.

For the past weeks of training, the transition from the trot into the walk was no longer executed by a sort of trailing off of the trot but by a definite transition in which the horse was pushed forward with both legs and made to step briskly under his body with the hind legs. Repeated short actions with the reins (half halts) made him pass in unaltered rhythm of the trot smoothly and supplely into the walk. The same accuracy is now demanded at the canter. The horse must not pass from the canter into the walk by performing steps of trot in between. As a preparation for this exercise, correct transitions from the trot into the walk are practiced as well as frequent changes of speed at the canter, which teach the horse a lively collected canter with elastic bounds. It is most important to remind the pupil that the collected canter is not obtained by pulling at the reins but mainly by bracing the back while pushing the horse forward with both legs. By increased aids of the legs the rider stimulates the horse's impulsion and by his braced back and repeated short actions of the reins causes the bounds of canter to become shorter until after five or six of these short bounds the horse passes smoothly into the walk with his hind legs well under him and without lying on the rein. In the same way the pupil must strike off directly and smoothly into the canter without any hasty steps of walk or trot in between.

As another step toward progress, the teacher now demands correct halts and walk in contact with the bit. So far, immediately after the transition into the walk the reins were given completely to provide a period of rest to the horse. Now the pupil tries to preserve also at the walk the impulsion he built up in the other paces. The horse should move at a pure, ordinary, or collected walk with regular strides and be ready upon the increased pressure of his rider's legs and corresponding slackening of the reins to pass into the extended walk without irregular steps or to change the pace in the correct manner as repeatedly described.

Again the teacher must be reminded to change the rein frequently in the course of the lesson. This is the moment to teach the simple change of leg at the canter. The teacher asks the pupil to canter across the diagonal and to pass into the walk six steps before reaching the long side of the school. After one or two steps at a pure walk he should strike off on the other leg. In the beginning the teacher may allow him to perform a larger number of steps and with increased skill in this exercise reduce the number to the prescribed one. Later the simple change of leg is performed on the diagonal at the center of the riding school. Various other possibilities of the change of rein at the canter, executed by a simple change of leg, will be described later.

Now that the rider has learned to perform the collected walk, the halt, which he learned before dismounting, is taught in the correct way. Again, the teacher chooses the easiest form of the exercise, that is, the halt from the walk. By repeated short half halts and the pushing aids of both legs the horse is brought to a standstill and made to place front and hind legs side by side, his weight distributed evenly on all four legs. Contact with the bit and position of the head must remain unaltered. The duration of the halt should be only gradually extended. The horse must slowly grow accustomed to carrying the rider's weight willingly at the standstill and not fidget on the spot. On principle, before bringing the lesson to an end the teacher should demand a correct halt from his pupil. If he does not succeed or the horse does not stand still, he should ride once more around the arena and try the correct halt again. The rider should not dismount before the horse has stood still for a while. Dismounting will then mean a reward for the horse, and the pupil learns to make it a habit to demand that his horse stand still before and after work.

When the halt from the walk presents no more problems, it is practiced from the working trot or the collected trot. In the interest of progress, the teacher must not allow his pupil to let the trot fade away gradually and with steps at the walk in between. The horse must step well under his body with the hind legs and stand straight with his weight on all four legs. He should not lose the contact with the bit nor lie on the rein. When the horse steps aside with one hind leg and performs a crooked halt, the rider's leg was not sufficiently firmly applied on this side. If the horse comes to a standstill on his forehand, the leg aids were ineffective. Moreover, a halt on the forehand is an undeniable sign that the rider's hand was too hard. Instead of a short giving and taking action of the reins, the pupil maintained a steady pull and prevented the hind legs from stepping under the body. Therefore, the rider should push the horse forward with both legs to maintain the collection and then reduce the speed by half halts with the reins while bracing his back. The horse must stand still, concentrated on his rider, and be prepared to pass immediately into the next movement demanded.

When the pupil has learned to ride his horse in balance in all exercises mentioned so far and is able to preserve his form in the various movements, that is, in contact with the bit and obedient, he is ready to learn the halt from the collected canter. Again the horse is expected to come to a standstill without making any steps of trot or walk in between but pass directly from the canter to the halt on all four legs. If the pupil succeeds he gives proof of a considerable degree of progress which deserves ample praise. This halt is the most difficult one to perform and demands very careful preparation. It is impossible to obtain before the pupil can perform correct transitions from the canter into the walk. This shows clearly what kind of preparation is necessary. With the pushing aids of both legs the rider stimulates the collected horse to perform lively bounds of canter. He must sit on the inside seat bone. The rein aids remain the same as when demanding the transition from the canter into the walk but the half halts must be administered more intensively. The horse must bring the canter to an end smoothly, stand in the direction of the movement with his fore and hind legs side by side and with his head in the correct position, and remain motionless.

Along with the canter fading away into the halt, another frequent fault occurs when the horse swings his hind quarters to the side, for instance, from the canter left to the left side. He becomes crooked and does not stand in the direction of the movement. This crookedness is partly the fault of the horse, who out of laziness tries to avoid the increased flexion of the hind legs which are supposed to step more under his body. On the other hand, it may be caused by the rider whose outside leg influences the horse too strongly and pushes the hind quarters to the side. Or, by a strong pull at the reins and insufficient pushing aids of the legs, the rider brings the horse to a hard and abrupt halt on the forehand. Apart from the fact that such a halt does not present a pleasant sight, the horse is unable to follow any further commands of his rider. In the interest of progress, however, the teacher must insist that the pupil strike off from the halt without any steps of walk or trot in between but performing a true bound of canter as the first movement from the standstill.

Riding straight lines lays a basis that is as beneficial to hacking as to dressage or jumping. The longer the lines the better the teacher may control whether his pupil does ride a straight line. As a change he demands various turns in between to keep the attention of horse and rider alert. One of these exercises is called "down the center." From the center of the short side of the school the rider turns his horse down the center line to the opposite short side, performing this turn exactly as when passing correctly through a corner. Here the turn is more difficult than in a corner where the walls meeting at right angles limit the horse's movement to the outside and prevent the hind quarters from falling out. In this turn the rider's outside leg behind the girth must keep the hind legs on the track. Three steps before reaching the center of the short side the rider's inside rein leads the horse onto the center line while the inside leg pushing on the girth bends the horse's body according to the arc of the circle and maintains the motion. The influence of the outside rein limits the position of the horse's head to the inside and, more important still, takes the horse after the turn—supported by the outside leg—straight and directly to the opposite side. The exercises "half the school" or "simple turns" (from one long side of the arena across the school to the opposite one or from the long side to the center line before dismounting) are performed in the same way. These exercises are easier than "down the center" as the straight line after the turn is a shorter one. All turns are performed at the walk and trot first and attempted at the canter when satisfactory at the two other paces.

Riding a volte (a small circle) is an increased demand on a pupil who knows how to execute correct circles and ride accurately through a corner. A perfect volte is a circle of six steps' diameter. It is an excellent exercise which increases the suppleness and obedience of the horse. By the same token, a volte correctly performed reveals a high degree of flexibility and balance in the horse that does not stiffen against the rider's hand but allows the action of the rein, affecting the hind leg of the same side, to influence his whole body correctly. If he does not have this degree of efficiency, the horse is unable to perform a circle of six steps' diameter without losing the rhythm and the regularity of his steps. Instead, he would very likely accelerate or slow down and produce an oval or many-sided figure.

It goes without saying that this exercise is performed at the trot, as a volte at the canter demands much more skill of horse and rider and should not be attempted until much later. It is easier for the pupil to execute the volte in a corner, and in the beginning the teacher may allow him to describe a somewhat larger circle. In a corner the first half of the circle is limited by the walls of the school. The pupil must try to continue the second half just as round. The inside rein leads the horse into the volte. The inside leg on the girth bends the horse according to the size of the circle and maintains rhythm and motion which should not alter. The outside rein, which must never be neglected, defines the size of the volte and the degree of the position. This rein prevents the horse from bending his neck too much into the volte, which the teacher must particularly watch out for. The outside leg is placed behind the girth. It bends the horse's body around the rider's inside leg and prevents the hind quarters from swinging to the outside, which is a severe fault. The teacher should warn the pupil against sliding to the outside with his seat which would encourage the horse's hind quarters to fall out and deviate from the circle.

The teacher has an excellent means of testing the correctness of a volte: he makes sure that both reins lie evenly alongside the horse's neck. When, for instance, the right rein does not touch the horse's neck and the left one is pressed firmly against it and the rider's left hand crosses over the horse's mane to the other side, the teacher may conclude that the horse makes himself hollow on the right side (taking an exaggerated position of head and neck to this side) and stiff on the other. On no account should he allow his pupil to continue practicing such incorrect voltes but order him to go back to the correct preparation of this exercise. The pupil must again practice riding correct turns and corners and execute them as well as circles mainly to the stiff side. When changing the speed he reduces the tempo by executing half halts on the stiff side while the rein of the hollow side remains applied. Special attention must be paid to see that the horse takes an even contact on the bit on both sides. With both reins applied evenly the horse accepts the bit on the stiff side and on the other follows the action of the rein by bending his neck to this side, making his neck hollow. With the rein of the hollow side applied, the pupil administers short half halts on the stiff side until the horse relaxes on this side—nodding, so to speak, and thus accepting the rein on the hollow side.

The volte may also be prepared on the circle, a method especially useful with unskilled riders. In this case the circle is gradually decreased in size by performing a spiral to a circle slightly larger than a volte (eight to ten steps' diameter). This gives horse and rider the opportunity to get accustomed to a smaller circle. The aids are the same as those described for the volte but begin lightly with a gradually increased effect. The teacher insists that the horse not slow down with the decreasing of the circle and lose his rhythm. After two or three rounds on this smaller circle the horse is led back onto the large circle by the outside rein performing another spiral. Again it must be emphasized that in the interest of training it is preferable to ride a somewhat larger volte correctly than to observe the prescribed size but ride it odd-shaped and with loss of rhythm.

The importance of frequent changes of rein has been repeatedly pointed out and should be stressed once more to prevent one-sidedness in the pupil and to develop both sides of the horse evenly. In the early stages the change of rein was executed mainly over the diagonal of the school, but now the teacher may make use of several other possibilities and thus render the lesson more lively and interesting as well as increasing his demands on horse and rider. When changing over the diagonal in this more advanced phase, the pupil passes the corner to the long side and after exactly six steps leaves the track and takes his horse in a straight line to the opposite long side, reaching the track exactly six steps before the corner. Such correctness reveals to the teacher that it is the rider who leads his horse and does not through laziness allow him to follow his own will, in which case the horse would probably begin to sway on the diagonal. The horse needs three steps to pass correctly through the corner if observing the radius demanded by the classical rules. After the corner and for straightening before turning on the diagonal, three more steps are necessary. The same number of steps is needed to turn from the diagonal on to the opposite track and through the corner.

Another means of changing the rein is the "change through the circle." This exercise is particularly important when working on the circle for a length of time. It offers an opportunity to develop both sides of the horse evenly. The horse describes a half circle from the circumference to the center of the large circle. In the center his position is changed, that is, his inside rein now becomes the outside one. He is then taken in a half circle of the same size on the other rein back to the large circle to a point exactly opposite from where he started. This exercise also offers an opportunity to increase the horse's attention as well as his suppleness and obedience.

Another change of rein may be executed after the exercise "down the center" or a turn across the school. These turns were minutely explained earlier in this book but now are followed by a change of rein when reaching the opposite wall.

When the pupil has mastered the volte he will have little difficulty changing the rein by a "half volte and change." This variation of the volte is another means of increasing the horse's attention to the rider's aids. Having performed a half volte, the rider leads his horse on a straight line at an angle of 45 degrees back to the track from which he started. Arriving at the track he changes the position of the horse. This exercise begins with the same aids as used for the volte. On completion of the half volte, the outside rein interrupts the circular movement and takes the horse back to the wall on a straight line. While the outside leg remained passive behind the girth during the volte, it is now placed on the girth to make the horse straight. Both legs push him forward on a single track and prevent him from becoming crooked.

Two more possibilities of changing the rein are provided by the exercises "turn on the forehand" and "turn on the haunches." For the turn on the forehand the horse must come to a halt and stand still with his weight placed evenly on all four legs. By the pressure of the outside leg behind the girth the rider makes the horse turn step by step around the forelegs which move on the spot until he comes again to a standstill in the opposite direction. The turn on the forehand can be executed from the halt only and never along the wall where the horse would not have sufficient room for his head and neck. The teacher should remember that the turn on the forehand is only a means to make the pupil or a young horse understand the yielding to the leg (following the pressure of the leg by moving into the opposite direction). It is by no means an exercise to be practiced assiduously, as it is of no practical value to the training. At liberty a horse does not turn on the forehand but on the haunches or on his middle.

The turn on the haunches, on the other hand, is executed whenever a quick turn in restricted space is necessary. It is the shortest and quickest means to change the rein and the smallest turn that can be made at the walk. The smallest turn at the canter is called a half pirouette. When the horse is at the trot he must be taken into the walk before the turn on the haunches, and after completion of the exercise, taken into the trot again. From the halt the horse must move off as into the walk. As soon as he lifts his legs from the ground he is turned around his hind quarters and then must come to a standstill again. The turn on the haunches may be practiced alongside the wall. The forehand describes a half circle around the hind legs which move on the spot. The inside hind foot treads on the spot at the rhythm of the walk. It is the center of a small half circle which is described by the outside hind leg. This exercise together with the halt and the rein-back concludes this phase of training. It may never be called correct when the inside hind leg remains riveted to the ground while the other leg is lifted once or twice at the utmost. The teacher must impress upon the pupil that during the turn on the haunches the rhythm of the walk must not be interrupted.

The inside rein leads the forehand into the turn while the inside leg on the girth gives the horse the lateral bend to the inside and maintains the legs in motion, preventing them from stepping back, which is a severe fault. The outside rein is slightly applied and limits the degree of the position of the head, preventing the horse from throwing himself into the turn. The outside leg is placed behind the girth to give the signal to turn around the inside hind leg, and together with the inside leg, interferes immediately if the horse tries to move backwards.

The instructor should not attempt to teach the rein-back before the pupil's progress has become obvious in the way he masters his horse, rides him smoothly and harmoniously, and fluently performs the various exercises explained so far, including halts from the different paces. To begin with, the teacher contents himself with one or two steps of rein-back and should not commit the mistake of demanding too many from his pupil right away. This mistake would lead to the horse resisting the action of the rein (which very likely was a prolonged pull) and moving backwards reluctantly, even dragging his feet. It is with unaltered position of his head and without losing collection and becoming longer in his body that the horse must move backwards on a straight line and without faltering, lifting the diagonal legs simultaneously off the ground and setting them down again at the same time. The movement must not become hasty or irregular.

Before the rein-back the horse should stand correctly on all four legs. He is then asked to move on at the walk by both legs pushing on the girth, the rider giving the reins only very slightly. As soon as the horse begins the movement he is made to step back by repeated short actions of the reins. The rider's legs remain applied to the girth and increase their pressure if the horse begins to creep back. They also enable the rider to interrupt the rein-back or make the horse move forward. The horse should be able to perform the transition into the walk immediately from the rein-back as well as break into the trot or strike off into the canter. When reining back correctly, the horse bends the three joints of his hind legs deeply, which improves their suppleness. Therefore, it is easier for the horse to strike off into the canter from the rein-back than from the halt. The teacher should remember this fact and use it for instruction.

Having mastered satisfactorily the exercises enumerated in this chapter, the pupil gives proof of an advanced degree of skill and accomplishment which, according to the standard of general riding, allows him to call himself a good rider. From the standpoint of dressage, he is ready for the difficult exercises. The duration of time in which this level of training may be reached depends mainly on the talent of the rider and the time he may spend on his training every day. A beginner should expect to spend at least six months to one year to arrive at this level. Again it is not the length of time that determines the accomplishment but the degree of skill, especially with regard to the correctness of the performance.

As we've said, the discussion of training for the highest demands of dressage surpasses the object of this book and will not be included here. However, with a particularly ambitious and gifted pupil who has great interest in dressage, the instructor may endeavor to develop his abilities further and take him to the threshold of the art of riding, provided that he has available a well-trained school horse who may teach the pupil the feeling of the difficult exercises. Without such an assistant the teacher would merely deceive himself and his pupil. As a conclusion to this chapter, lateral work (two tracks) and counter canter, which take the pupil to a higher level, will be explained.

The term lateral work is applied to the following exercises: shoulder-in, travers or quarters-in, half pass, renvers or tail to the wall, and full travers or full pass. Half pass and renvers may be performed in all three paces; shoulder-in and quarters-in in walk and trot only. The full travers, which is rarely practiced nowadays, is always begun from the halt and comes to an end again with a halt. The full travers was in practical use when the armies had cavalries and the riders had to correct the distance between each other during parades. In lateral work the sequence of steps of all three paces remains unchanged but the horse moves forward and sideways crossing his legs.

The most important exercise on two tracks is the shoulder-in, invented by the French riding master de la Guérinière in 1733. This exercise is the backbone for the training in the other lateral work and, besides, it is of decisive importance for straightening the horse. For the shoulder-in the forehand is taken into the arena about half a step and describes a separate line of hoofprints parallel to the wall while the hind quarters remain on the track along the wall. The inside fore-leg crosses over the outside one and the inside hind leg steps more in the direction of the horse's center of gravity. This means an increase of suppleness and flexion of this hind leg and makes the shoulders freer in their movement.

The teacher demands this exercise at the walk at first, because in this pace it is easier for the pupil to apply the aids correctly. Moreover, it gives the teacher more time to administer the necessary advice and corrections. Later it should be practiced mainly at the trot. The teacher must remember in the beginning to be satisfied with a few steps of shoulder-in executed correctly. In shoulder-in, especially when performed at the walk, the horse loses much impulsion, which the young rider cannot yet make up for by his pushing aids. When those few steps of shoulder-in are executed correctly and are well established, the demands may be increased gradually to longer periods of this exercise. In the interest of training of horse and rider, the teacher must, as always, be governed by the principle that a few steps well performed are of greater educational value than a larger number executed badly.

The inside rein takes the horse's shoulder away from the wall while the outside rein remains applied, otherwise the horse would just bend his neck to the inside without taking the shoulder away from the wall. The outside rein also leads the horse into the desired direction. One rein must not be used without the other. The inside leg with a deep knee and a low heel is applied on the girth and bends the horse from the poll to the tail to the inside, making the inside legs cross over the outside ones. The rider's outside leg is applied behind the girth preventing the hind quarters from swinging to the outside, which would annul the training value of the exercise. Both legs must maintain the horse in motion and he must not slow down. The rider's weight is shifted to the inside seat bone. Contrary to other lateral work, in the shoulder-in the position of the horse is not in the direction of his movement and he does not look into the direction in which he is going.

When the result is satisfactory at the walk, the exercise may be performed at the collected trot, again beginning with a few steps. Observations I have made in various riding establishments cause me to stress the fact that shoulder-in as well as the other lateral exercises may be performed at the collected trot only and never at the working trot, much less at the ordinary trot. Therefore, the horse must be capable of performing the collected trot before the lateral work may be begun.

It is advisable, especially when executing shoulder-in at the trot, to begin the exercise after having passed a corner of the school. The horse is led through the corner as if for a volte. When the forehand has moved away from the wall after the corner to continue the circle, the inside leg increases the pressure and the outside rein takes the horse in the shoulder-in along the wall.

Travers or quarters-in is of lesser importance to the

training than shoulder-in and is used equally to bend the hind legs and increase the lateral flexion of the horse's body. In this exercise the forehand remains on the track without, however, losing the position of head and neck to the inside, which is obtained by the aid of the inside rein while the outside rein leads the horse along the wall. The inside leg is applied on the girth, pushing the horse forward and, together with the inside rein and the outside leg, ensures the even lateral bend of the horse's body. The outside leg applied behind the girth makes the horse take his quarters away from the track and the outside hind leg step over the inside one.

Considering the inclination of most horses to go crooked, the practice of quarters-in should be limited to a minimum and in the interest of training be employed mainly as a preparation for the half pass. However, if a horse is especially stiff on one side, for instance on the left, resisting the lateral bend to this side, the practice of quarters-in on the left rein will considerably improve the insufficient lateral bend.

The half pass demonstrates best that lateral work consists of a forward and a sideways movement. The horse moves forward on an oblique line, his body parallel to the wall. The outside front and hind legs cross over in front of the inside ones. The forehand may somewhat precede the hind quarters but never vice versa. The position of head and neck and the lateral flexion of the horse's body point to the direction of the movement. This is obtained by the inside rein supported by the inside leg on the girth which also maintains the regular, fluent movement. The outside rein limits the degree of position and flexion and supports the inside rein in maintaining the desired direction. The outside leg behind the girth makes the horse step sideways and cross his outside legs over the inside ones. The rider's weight rests on his inside seat bone and his upper part must not remain behind the movement or lean to the outside. On the contrary, it should be shifted well into the direction of the movement.

The half pass may be performed on short lines, such as a half volte and half pass or a zigzag, on longer lines (half pass from the center line to the wall of the school or vice versa), and on long lines from one long side of the school to the opposite one. Considering the standard of the pupil discussed in this chapter, the half volte and half pass only may be taught, while the half pass on longer lines as well as the renvers belong to advanced training. The same applies to the half pass at the canter, which demands much more knowledge and skill than the student can possibly have acquired in the present stage.

For the half volte and half pass the pupil rides a half volte and then takes his horse on an oblique line in the half pass back to the track.

In the counter canter the horse canters on the right lead when, for instance, going on the left rein. The counter canter is an effective means of consolidating the horse's obedience and attention and of testing the correctness of his reaction to the rider's aids. At first the teacher should be satisfied when the pupil rides one long side of the school in the counter canter. Later he will demand that the rider remain in the counter canter through the corners. To begin with, the pupil is allowed to describe a larger arc when passing through the corners. Performing the counter canter through a corner of the correct small size demands greater experience and belongs in the sphere of advanced dressage. Besides, the horse, too, should be considerably advanced in his training. The counter canter is always a collected canter.

As we have said earlier in this chapter, teaching lateral work and counter canter should be considered as a mark of appreciation for particularly talented riders and prepare them eventually for further advanced training. Consequently, only a limited number of students may benefit from these lessons.

This chapter should not be concluded without a few words about the use of spur and double bridle. At the end of this first phase of training of a dressage horse, the curb bit may be applied and the rider begins to wear spurs. Intentionally, neither were mentioned so far, as their use is closely connected with the progressive demands made upon the horse as well as the increasing skill and proficiency of the rider. Therefore, using spurs and double bridle demands an individual method of instruction. Spurs are used before the double bridle while the horse is still in a snaffle and will be discussed first.

Spurs should not be used before the horse is sufficiently advanced in his training and the student has learned to sit independently in all situations—when he has literally won his spurs. The use of the spur is to intensify the leg aids of the rider and represents the last resort of the pushing aids. The spurs should be carefully selected according to the horse's temperament and sensitiveness and should never risk wounding his flanks. On no account should the teacher allow his pupil to wear sharp and pointed spurs, but should permit only those with a finely serrated wheel or, better still, a blunt knob. Traces of blood on the horse's body reveal a wrong or brutal use of this auxiliary aid and have repeatedly provoked indignant interference of onlookers as well as of the societies for prevention of cruelty to animals—not very flattering for the noble sport of riding.

The spurs are fastened to the boots in such a way that the rider may touch his horse near the girth without raising his heels. When instructing young pupils on phlegmatic horses that obey only sluggishly to the inefficient pushing aids of their riders, it may be advisable to introduce the students to the spurs in the early stages of systematic training (page 72.)

The situation is different during the basic training of a young horse. In this case the rider may use the spurs to reinforce his pushing aids only after appropriate progress has been obtained. The spurs are applied to the horse's flanks simultaneously with an increased leg aid and return to their original position as soon as the correct reaction to this aid has been obtained. When this is not the case, the aid of the spur is repeated. It must never be used sharply against the horse's body as it would no longer be an aid but a punishment.

The teacher must warn his pupil against too frequent use of the spur. He must impress upon him that the horse's sensitiveness would be blunted and that the rider would condemn himself to helplessness. Besides, the reason for unsteady contact with the bit and irregular movements of the horse, as well as twisting of the tail, is frequently to be sought in constant use of the spurs. Nor must the spurs be applied too far behind the girth, which might induce the horse to kick or adopt other bad habits.

We've repeatedly pointed out the eminent importance of the contact with the bit, which is fundamental for the entire training of a riding horse. Therefore, the correct bitting should be carefully observed from the very beginning. On page 29 the snaffle was explained; now the double bridle and its effect will be discussed.

The double bridle or curb consists of two parts: the curb bit and the snaffle. The curb comprises the mouthpiece with the curb chain and the headpiece, to the cheekpieces of which the bit is fastened. Another head- and cheekpiece goes with the snaffle. The effect of the curb bit is the more important one.

The severity of the double bridle depends on the thickness of the mouthpiece, the size of the port, and, finally, of the proportion of the upper cheek to the lower. It may also be regulated by the adjustment of the curb. When choosing a double bridle, the width of the horse's mouth must first be measured. If the mouthpiece is too narrow, the cheeks of the curb exert a pressure on the lips, pushing them into the horse's mouth, which causes discomfort and pain. On the other hand, a mouthpiece which is too wide will not lie well in the horse's mouth but will slide about from one side to the other with the actions of the reins.

As with the snaffle so with the curb, the thinner the mouthpiece, the sharper its effect, and the thicker, the milder. Consequently, for a horse with fleshy bars a thinner curb bit may be selected, and for one with sensitive bars, a thicker mouthpiece. With the port the fact has to be considered that an increase in size makes its effect more severe. Therefore, for a sensitive horse a bit with a low port is chosen which, however, must not be too low either. This would hinder the freedom of the tongue and disturb the correct contact. The proportion of the upper cheek to the lower is important, as it decides the lever action of the bit. A short upper cheek makes the effect more severe and so does a longer lower cheek. The more the length of upper and lower cheek equal each other, the milder the effect of the curb. As a rule, the lower cheek should at the utmost be twice as long as the upper one. With the curb chain, which gives the full effect to the curb bit, another possibility is given to regulate the severity of the double bridle. Thus the curb chain is more important than is generally assumed. It should be made of flat and large links. The pressure of the curb chain may induce a horse with a bony chin groove to throw his head up, which should be prevented by placing a leather or rubber pad under the chain. Special care should be taken that the chain lies evenly around the chin and does not touch it only in certain places which would cause discomfort to the horse. Fitting the whole headpiece carefully is equally important and should not be taken lightly. The cheekpieces must be adjusted long enough so that the mouthpiece does not touch the tush. With the mouthpiece lying lower—without touching the tush—the severity may be increased and made milder with the mouthpiece lying somewhat higher in the horse's mouth. The snaffle bit is placed above the mouthpiece of the curb near the corners of the mouth without, however, wrinkling the horse's lips.

The curb chain is hooked into the left curb hook and turned flat and placed into the right hook in such a way that with the reins applied, the lower cheek of the curb forms an angle of forty to forty-five degrees with the mouth of the horse. If this angle is wider, the curb chain is too loose and the curb becomes ineffective. With a smaller angle, the effect of the curb bit becomes too severe as the curb chain is too tight. It is the lesser fault to have the curb chain too loose, which is even recommended at times when using a double bridle on a young and sensitive horse for the first time. A cavesson noseband completes the double bridle and should be placed high enough not to pinch the horse's lips between the bit and the noseband.

The horse should accept both snaffle and double bridle quietly and with a closed mouth, the bit lying on his tongue. He should not open his mouth with the action of the rein. A moist or even foaming mouth gives proof of a steady contact with the bit as well as of the actions of the reins going through the body of the horse. A dry mouth is a bad sign, calling the teacher's attention to the horse's lack of suppleness or—more often—the hard hand of the rider.

Difficulties with the tongue, such as hanging it out or placing it over the bit, frequently occur together with an open mouth and should never be neglected, either with the snaffle or with the curb. Generally they come from pains in the mouth caused by incorrect bitting or by the clumsy hand of the rider. They may also be caused by pains in the hind quarters or, with nervous horses, by excitement. The best remedy for such problems is the immediate return to the early stages of training as explained in the previous chapters. If they occur when using a double bridle, training should continue in a snaffle.

The riding teacher must bear in mind that the change from the snaffle to the curb bit seriously affects the habits of both horse and rider, which must be taken into consideration during the lessons. The double bridle is a much more severe bit. Even with a school horse that had been introduced to the curb bit before and in between was ridden in a snaffle by a beginner, this fact must be taken into account. Therefore, to begin with the curb should be adjusted more loosely and the horse ridden well forward with the snaffle reins more applied than the curb reins. The impulsion built up during the training in the snaffle must be preserved by all means.

When changing from the snaffle to the double bridle, the pupil must adapt himself to guiding his horse with four reins —curb reins and snaffle reins. It is to the student's advantage to at least explain to him the classical way of holding the reins, today often called "three in one." The right hand holds one rein and the left, three. When mounting, the curb rein is left lying on the horse's neck and the rider mounts, using the snaffle rein as was explained on pages 40–41. When in the saddle, he takes both curb reins in his left hand, separating them by the third finger, and shortens them with his right hand until the contact with the bit is established. The left snaffle rein is taken into the same hand, separated from the left curb rein by the little finger. The right snaffle rein is passed between the little and the third finger of the right hand (as when riding in a snaffle alone) and applied. The left hand is formed into a fist and carried with a rounded wrist in front of the middle of the body just above the pommel of the saddle. The right hand is held near the left one, the ends of

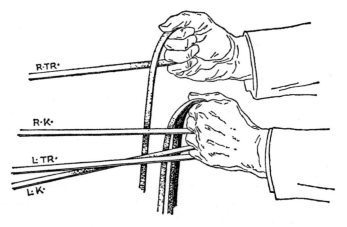

Correct way of holding reins of the double bridle:
R.TR.=right snaffle rein; R.K.=right curb rein;
L.TR.=left snaffle rein; L.K.=left curb rein

the reins hanging freely between the right snaffle rein and the right side of the horse's neck. It is important that all four reins should be evenly applied; therefore, the rider must correct the length of the reins with his right hand in the course of his lesson. When riding with a double bridle, the rider is to wear spurs and always hold the whip in his right hand.

For the action of the left rein or a left turn, the left hand with the three reins is turned to the right in such a way that the little finger points toward the right hip of the rider. Meanwhile the right hand gives the right snaffle rein by a slight turn to the front. The action of the right rein is obtained by a turn of the left hand to the left, the little finger moving somewhat away from the rider's body. At the same time the right hand is turned to the left, the little finger directed toward the rider's left hip.

For some time since the F.E.I. declared the way of holding the reins "optional," the inventiveness of riders has created a number of different ways to guide a riding horse, mostly consisting of separating the curb reins and holding them together with the snaffle reins, that is, left curb and left snaffle reins in the left hand and right curb and right snaffle reins in the right hand. This kind of guidance causes the horse to take a much stronger contact with the bit, especially when the rider separates his hands, holding them at a distance from each other. As a consequence, the horse loses the suppleness in his reactions to the rein aids which the rider can no longer apply in delicate nuances. Furthermore, it becomes a problem to guide the horse with one hand, though this should be one of the main objects in riding, the distant goal, as it were, of the schooling of a riding horse. It is the classical way of holding the reins—three in one—that permits the rider to guide the horse delicately with one hand. In fact, in the past century this technique was obligatory in most European cavalry schools.

The effect of the double bridle being so much more severe, it demands an especially light hand and much sensitiveness and tact on the part of the rider. For this reason the riding teacher should allow the use of the curb bit only upon mature consideration to those pupils who are particularly talented and working toward a higher goal, and only when they prepare themselves to participate in a competition. After the show, the snaffle should be used again and it should by all means be given preference for the daily work.

13. On a horse that is not fully trained
(the pupil's own horse)

As repeatedly noted, the present-day instructor rarely has a correctly and fully trained school horse at his disposal.

However, this fact should not discourage an ambitious riding teacher. On the contrary, it should stimulate him to work toward the goal of pages 109–10 by adapting his method to the given situation. The result depends on the talent of the pupil and the progress he has achieved so far as well as on the abilities of the horse and his level of training.

We now deal with the advanced training of a pupil on his own horse or a riding horse that is not fully schooled but has reached the standard of training as set forth on pages 68ff. The general lines of instruction are the same as for that on a school horse, but a considerably longer period of time must be calculated to obtain a similar result. As not only the rider but also the horse must learn and progress, the instructor should ride the horse himself frequently to introduce him to new exercises or to eradicate faults. He must take special care to increase his demands step by step and to build on a sound foundation. Many explanations already given in the previous chapter are here repeated for the sake of clarity and completeness and as a convenience for reference.

So far the main object of the lessons was to consolidate the pupil's seat and improve the horse's impulsion. Consequently, details such as strictly observing the straight track were generously overlooked. From this point on, however, the teacher insists that the pupil guide his horse with greater precision. After having ridden the horse mainly forward on straight lines to increase his impulsion, work on the circle now comes to the foreground. Here it is easier for the pupil to guide his horse correctly while maintaining his seat. Also, he applies the aids more effectively. But it is advisable to alternate work on the circle with going large at intervals in order to re-establish the necessary impulsion. Now the teacher demands that the pupil remain strictly on the track. This is easier alongside a solid wall than in an open arena marked out by letters or symbols at the corners and sides. The teacher should therefore not reprimand his pupil harshly when he leaves an undulating track in the open arena after having ridden straight along the wall in the indoor school. It is preferable to work indoors or along a solid fence until the pupil has learned to ride a straight line. At a later stage, however, he should learn to ride parallel to the wall at a distance of two to four steps. This exercise is an increased demand for which horse and rider must gradually acquire the ability and which is of value only when the horse is actually able to go a straight line parallel to the wall and does not sway or falter. This is what the teacher must watch out for.

Before attempting this exercise, however, the pupil should learn to ride correctly through the corners of the school. In the past period the main object was to build up impulsion and to make work more lively, so the horse was allowed to pass through the corners on a larger or smaller arc of a circle as he pleased. Now the pupil must take his horse through the corner on an arc of a circle of a given size. A horse will usually try to describe a larger curve, which is easier for him because he bends his inside hind leg less than on a small one. In most riding establishments of less than top standards, the observation may be made that it is hardly ever the rider who takes his horse through a corner but the horse that chooses his own way and becomes irritated when being disturbed. From the hoofprints in the sand it may be seen that the horse does not follow a straight line along the short side of the school but describes a large curve touching the wall for a short moment. Furthermore he throws himself into the turn, leaning on his shoulder. Arriving at the corner or even before reaching it, the horse becomes crooked as he prepares to avoid the effort of the increased flexion. A corner of that sort is of no value for the training of horse and rider. For the correct exercise the horse must pass through the corner on an arc of a circle of six steps' diameter. His body should be bent in such a way that his spine corresponds to the arc of the circle. Consequently he must be taken onto the curve three steps before reaching the corner and arrive at the new wall again three steps after the corner. This description of a correct corner represents the ideal of perfection which the rider approaches at moments and misses at others. It is important for both teacher and pupil to be well aware of this fact. Furthermore, the teacher should be able to classify the degree of correctness of a performance as to its value and give his reasons and, if it was bad, find the effective remedy. With riding, much more important than recognizing the fault is to find the cause. The teacher should beware of demanding that the exercise be performed strictly according to the classical rules right from the beginning. At this stage of training the horse might too easily lose his balance and the regularity of his steps. Therefore, at first the rider passes through the corner on a somewhat larger arc, gradually decreasing its size when the horse has learned to maintain unaltered the regularity and the tempo of his movement.

The hind legs should follow exactly the tracks of the forefeet, and the hind quarters should not swing to the outside or to the inside. A corner correctly passed represents an excellent test for horse and rider. The rider learns to lead his horse into the corner with the outside rein without the horse taking a position to the outside. With the inside rein he takes him through the corner and onto the straight line. With his outside leg behind the girth he prevents the hind quarters from falling out. Many horses will try to throw their quarters to the outside to avoid the inconvenience of bending the body and the inside hind leg. The rider's inside leg on the girth pushes the horse forward and maintains the fluent movement. When passing correctly through the corner the horse is bent in an increased measure and becomes more supple and skilled. His reactions to the aids of reins and legs become keener, and any inclination to laziness or bad habits is effectively nipped in the bud. Demanding the performance of correct corners should not be cast aside as a sort of academic fussiness but be recognized as a valuable means of schooling which measures precisely the level of training reached.

Having progressed to this point, the teacher will once more make sure that the horse moves straight and correct him if necessary. Many a riding horse does move on a straight line, though the hind legs do not follow the tracks of the forelegs but step to the side, and so the horse is crooked. The crookedness of the horse is not only a bad habit but also and above all a serious fault which has a negative effect on the future training of horse and rider.

At liberty a horse rarely moves crooked. Under the weight of the rider, however, most young horses and many old and incorrectly trained ones adopt the habit of placing their hind quarters away from the wall and into the arena. Their hind legs no longer step in the direction of the hoofprints of the forelegs. To some extent this is due to the fact that a horse is narrower through the shoulders than through the hind quarters. If the outside part of the body (shoulders and hips) remains parallel to the wall or the horse leans toward the wall with his shoulder, seeking support, his hind legs necessarily must step farther into the arena than the forelegs. The cause of crookedness is frequently to be sought in incorrect or forcible methods of schooling. It may also be proof that the horse has been rushed in his training.

If the teacher aims at serious progress and success with his pupil he must set to work to eliminate this bad habit, which is not easy to do but of eminent importance for the entire training. By pushing his shoulder toward the wall the horse tries to evade the guidance of his rider and simultaneously avoids the flexion of the three joints of his hind legs which are the motor of locomotion necessary for a riding horse. Consequently the gymnastic training of the hind quarters becomes impossible and there is no development of suppleness, which means no elastic swinging back, no regularity and rhythm of the movements, no ability to increase the tempo.

It would be a waste of time and energy if the teacher continued to work with his pupil as he did before when there were intermediate goals to be reached without teaching him now to straighten his horse. Straighten means to take the shoulder of the horse away from the wall and bring it in front of the hind quarters. The shoulder must be brought in until the hind legs no longer step to the side of the forefeet but in their hoofprints. It is with both reins and simultaneous pushing aids of the legs that the shoulder is brought in. The rein aids without the pushing aids would make the horse reduce his speed. A horse can be straightened only when he remains in unaltered movement during the correction. It is especially necessary for the teacher to see that the pupil does not try to take the forehand in with the inside rein alone without applying the outside one. The result would be an increased position of the horse's head to the inside but not a straight horse. A teacher who has the absurd idea of telling his pupil to straighten his horse by pushing his hind quarters to the outside of the track with his inside leg has grasped neither the essence of riding nor the anatomy of the horse.

At this stage the exercises "from the wall to the wall" and "serpentines along the wall" help to straighten the horse as well as increase his suppleness and obedience. If the horse leans toward the wall with his shoulder, trying to evade the inside rein and fight the straightening, the exercise "from the wall to the wall" is particularly recommended. Having passed through the second corner of the short side of the school the horse is taken on a straight line to the center of the arena where his position is changed. He is then taken again on a straight line back to the same wall sufficiently far from the corner to enable him to pass it easily.

Simple or double serpentines along the wall have similar effect with a horse that is already more advanced in his training. He is led away from the wall and back to it in the manner just described, with the difference that he is not taken to the center but to an imaginary line parallel to the wall and about five meters away from it for the simple serpentine and at a distance of three meters for the double one.

Having well consolidated the work of the young horse at the walk and trot, the teacher may begin work at the canter as explained on pages 82–83 and 110–11. At first it is practiced on the circle and later on the straight line with transitions from the trot. It is more important to concentrate on the precise execution of the exercise than to repeat it thoughtlessly too often. When going large around the entire school the strike-off is easier for the horse in the corners than on a straight line.

The periods of rest interspersed in the lesson may be used to practice halts and standing still, exercises of which any riding horse should be capable. Riding straight up to a determined point helps to increase the attention of horse and rider. All exercises enumerated here should be practiced in all three paces, walk, trot, and canter. Work at the trot, however, takes up the largest part of the training because in this pace it is easier than at the canter for the pupil to maintain the correct seat and consequently apply the correct aids. Also, the trot is better suited than any other pace to make the horse supple and flexible. The correct performance of turns, voltes, and halts from all three paces and moving on again, rein-back, simple change of leg at the canter, and turn on the haunches should be taught as described on pages 109ff.

Once more the riding teacher is reminded that in the present case he deals with two pupils at a time, horse and rider. Contrary to the situation discussed previously, the horse must learn, himself, and this different situation requires the frequent active assistance (or interference) of the teacher (i.e., he must ride the horse). This means a longer period of training but still the horse may not achieve the standard of a school or dressage horse schooled through years by an experienced rider.

Let us once more emphasize the most important points of a good dressage horse: he should move forward with impulsion, which shows best when he is able to remain on a straight line. This impulsion, fundamental to the entire training, is not present in a horse that sways and goes crooked or in one that proceeds with hurried and hasty steps. Lack of rhythm means lack of balance, which is just as necessary for riding as for dancing. In this case it is much more important for the training to concentrate on the correct movement of the horse than to practice various exercises. Changes of pace, trot and canter especially, as well as those of speed are the best means to cultivate the physical balance of the horse until in the transitions from one pace or speed into the other he does not become hasty or hurried, or lose the rhythm of the movement, or come on his forehand, but remains supple and smooth. When the horse throws his shoulder into a turn or a volte or tilts his head, he gives proof of a lack of balance and suppleness. When a horse is relaxed he will move with a steady contact on the bit and with the correct position of his head which he should maintain through all phases of his movement. When carrying his rider in this way, a horse gives proof not only of his attention and willing submission to his rider but also of his absolute physical and mental balance. Mental balance, especially, is decisive for progress with highly bred and nervous animals. Experience has taught us, however, that a rider who by his seat and calm guidance does not disturb the balance may find in such a horse more than in others a loyal companion whose originally difficult temperament may never be suspected. Here is the best proof of the close relation of physical and mental balance as well as of the importance of the independent seat of the rider.

The further course of training is the same as that described earlier and, beyond pointing again to the longer duration of training, does not need any further explanation. The use of the spur has been discussed, but the change from the snaffle to the double bridle needs to be completed by additional details.

On page 132 we dealt with a horse that had been introduced to the double bridle at previous times and was to be readjusted. Now a young horse is to be made familiar with the curb bit, which demands much more delicacy. The bit must be selected with particular care and taking into account its severity and the sensitiveness of the horse's mouth. During the first few days of work with the new bit, the behavior of the horse should be studied and the curb readjusted if necessary. If unsteady contact or coming off the bit, open mouth, and difficulties with the tongue appear with a horse that was accustomed to take a quiet contact on a snaffle bit, it becomes obvious that he feels uncomfortable and that the curb bit needs to be checked and readjusted as to its size, severity, and fitting. If, however, the horse did not take a steady contact on the bit even when in a snaffle, he is simply not ready for the curb bit. It is a grave mistake of the riding teacher to put the horse in a double bridle so that the pupil might be able to present him in a better form. It is just as bad and objectionable as to try to force the horse's head into the required position by means of running reins. The horse must never be worked from the front to the rear but must be formed from the rear forward. Besides, he should feel at ease in order to follow willingly the demands of his rider, and the correct bitting is an important part of his comfort.

When there are no problems with the contact, on principle for the first few days of going in a double bridle the horse is ridden briskly forward and preferably at the rising trot to teach him to take the correct contact with this much more severe bit. The horse's impulsion, built up during work in a snaffle, must not be lost. In the beginning it is even advisable for the pupil to guide his horse with the snaffle reins leaving the curb reins loose, in spite of the double bridle. Thus the teacher makes it easier for both horse and rider to adjust to the new bit as already explained on page 132. Besides becoming accustomed to the more severe bit, the horse should learn to keep two bits—more steel—in his mouth. He might be easily tempted to open his mouth or to play with the bit with his tongue, which is the beginning of most difficulties with the tongue. The rider must now learn to calculate the much more severe action of the reins and try to guide his horse with a very light hand. Moreover, he has to deal with the problem of having four reins in his hands. With gradual progress all four reins should be evenly applied, and this must constantly be controlled and corrected. One or the other of the reins begins to slide from the rider's hand, especially when he does not fully close his fingers or when the horse becomes unsteady in his contact. The rein loses its effect, which is particularly bad when the curb reins are more firmly applied than the snaffle reins. Correcting the length of the reins is easier when riding "three in one," because the right hand holding the right snaffle rein only can comfortably adjust the three other reins to their correct length.

Once more, when riding a horse in a double bridle for the first time the order is: forward! In the beginning the pupil was permitted to lead his horse with the snaffle reins alone for the first few rounds. But now he shortens the curb reins gradually and brings them into contact with the horse's mouth. It is most important during this operation that the horse does not slow down in his movement. Any change of speed is a warning to the teacher that the horse is losing impulsion and becoming reluctant to go forward while the very opposite is the aim during the entire training. For this reason, lateral work should not be ridden with a horse that is being introduced to the double bridle, and the collected paces should be limited to very short periods. It is much more advisable to practice changes of speed at first in transitions from the ordinary trot to the extended trot and vice versa. Work at the canter follows the same pattern.

Training continues in approximately the same order as when riding in a snaffle: that is, all stages of training as explained on pages 109–43 have to be repeated. Horse and rider must learn all exercises once again in a double bridle, but the time necessary may be condensed to a minimum. The teacher should never forget to insist on the forward movement.

The more painstaking and time-consuming work which goes into the training of a green horse is made up for by an even greater pleasure and satisfaction. There is nothing more gratifying for the pupil than riding his own and self-trained horse correctly, and no greater reward for the instructor than the joyful progress of both his pupils—horse and rider.

14. Protocol and school figures

It appears necessary to summarize the traditional regulations of behavior in a riding school developed by generations of riders and to discuss them from today's standpoint in order to pass them on to the younger generations and thus assure their continuance. Such protocol is the result of experience gained in practice and should not be discarded as undue stress on rules and forms. It would be equally foolish to try to throw overboard the various approved rules in human life, as, for instance, traffic regulations. Just as such rules are made for the benefit of each individual, so does the protocol of a riding school allow each rider to work his horse in the arena without getting in the way of other riders and without being disturbed or hindered himself. This mutual consideration allows the activities of a riding school to run smoothly and should be dictated by self-evident equestrian tact. In short, such regulations have nothing to do with an obsolete formalism.

Few riders are lucky enough nowadays to be able to work their horses alone but have to share the riding hall or the open arena with other riders. For this reason the majority of properly run riding establishments has set up the most important regulations of conduct—rules of the house, as it were—which are more or less the same in most countries.

The rider upon entering the arena must make sure that he does not disturb other riders already at work. Particularly when the riding hall is crowded he asks permission to enter or leave with the question "Entrance clear?" or some other agreed-upon expression. On no account must he burst into the arena without paying attention to the other riders, which might cause a collision and entail serious accidents. The same rule must be observed when the rider leads his horse in or has him led in by the groom to mount in the arena. In this case, as has been repeatedly explained, the horse is taken into the middle of the school parallel to the short side, where the rider mounts without disturbing the others. A brief salute to those present is demanded by the most basic good manners. As the school is a place for riding, conversations should be limited to a minimum and never indulged in with a loud voice or on a subject other than riding.

The right of way to remain on the track along the wall is accorded to a rider who rides on a determined rein. In most countries it is the rider on the left rein who has priority, and it is from this standpoint that the rules of the school are discussed here. When two riders meet, the one riding on the right rein gives way in time by taking his horse from the track and remaining one or two steps away from the wall and parallel to it until the following corner. Riders practicing the walk should ride away from the track at a distance sufficient for the other riders working in the faster paces to pass each other comfortably. Overtaking is considered bad manners and is to be avoided in all circumstances. The rider in the faster pace coming up behind the slower one does not close up but turns away from the track and across the school to the other long side. The large circle is to be performed in such a way that there remains sufficient room for the other riders to pass each other comfortably on the track.

On principle, only those figures which were explained in the previous chapters and which are internationally approved are practiced in a school, especially when crowded. They are to be ridden as precisely as possible, and teacher and fellow students should be able to recognize them. The rider should not become so absorbed in his work that he does not see more of the school than the ears of his horse. On the contrary, his eyes should take in the whole arena, not only because looking down is considered a fault from the equestrian standpoint but also because he must be able to register the movements of the other riders in time and act accordingly.

For the sake of clarity here is a summary of the exercises and figures belonging to the standard of riding discussed in this book:

"Go large" means ride on straight lines along the walls of the school. Special care should be taken to ride the corners precisely on an arc of a circle of three steps' diameter. With very young horses and when riding in the extended paces, the corners may be performed somewhat larger.

"Half the school" (diagram) means to turn right or left from the center of the long side to the opposite wall, thus dividing the school into two sections.

The "Change through the diagonal" (diagram) is performed by riding a straight line from one long side of the school to the other. Six steps after the corner of the short side the horse is taken diagonally to the opposite long side arriving six steps before reaching the corner.

When "Changing through the half school" the horse is taken six steps after the corner of the short side diagonally to the center of the opposite long side.

Simple turns as "Left or right turn" are executed from the long sides. The horse is turned away from the wall on an arc of a circle of three steps' diameter and taken straight to the opposite long side where he continues on the same rein after performing another tight turn of three steps' diameter.

"Down the center" or "Down the center line" is a simple turn from the center of the short side to the opposite one.

After a simple turn as well as after "Down the center," the rein may be changed upon command of the teacher when reaching the opposite side. In this case he commands "Down the center and change" (diagram).

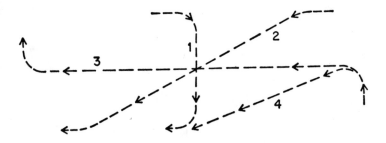

1. Half the school; 2. Change through the diagonal; 3. Down the center and change; 4. Change direction from the center line

The "Circle" (diagram) may be performed on either of the half sections of the school. It should have a diameter of sixteen to eighteen meters and leave sufficient room for the riders working along the track. When a rider works alone in the arena he may use the full width of the school, increasing the size of the circle until it touches the center of the short side and both long sides, having a diameter of twenty meters. The larger the circle, the easier for the horse; and the smaller, the more difficult. A smaller circle makes increased demands on the horse's suppleness and balance.

There are two ways to change the rein when working on the circle. "Change the circle in a figure of eight" (diagram) is the easier method. When the horse going on the circle reaches the center of the arena, his position is changed and another large circle is performed in the other half of the school on the other rein, thus describing a figure of eight. The second way is to "Change within the circle" (diagram), which requires less space and is therefore practiced more frequently. When crossing the center line or one of the points where the circle touches the long sides of the school or comes near them, the horse is taken in a half circle to the center where his position is changed. He is then led back on the

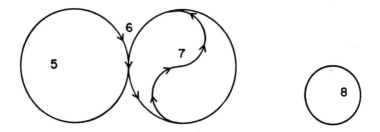

5. Circle; 6. Change the circle in a figure of eight; 7. Change within the circle; 8. Volte

other rein to a point on the circumference of the circle exactly opposite from where he started, thus describing the figure of half an eight within the circle. The pupil rides on the circle until the command "Go large" is given.

For the figure "From the wall to the wall" (diagram) the horse is taken after the corner of the short side in a straight line and on a single track to the center of the ring, where his position is changed. He is then led back in the same manner to the same long side of the school.

A "volte" (diagram) is the smallest circle that a horse is able to perform. It should be of six steps' diameter and may be executed in the corners as well as along the walls or on the center line. Contrary to the circle, the volte is performed once only and a repetition must be required expressly by the command "Double volte."

As the circle may be reduced to ten meters' diameter for the sake of practice, as is the case in a figure of eight, so the volte may be enlarged to eight meters' diameter, which is even required in some international dressage tests. The larger size of a volte must be explicitly demanded because otherwise it should be no larger than six steps' or six meters' diameter. This insignificant difference in measurements is due to the international rules which are sometimes based on steps and sometimes on meters.

The "Figure of eight" (diagram) is performed on the short side of the school between the two long sides. In the corner of the short side an enlarged volte or reduced circle of ten meters' diameter is ridden on, for instance, the left rein. When crossing the center line, the horse's position is changed and another circle described on the other rein, on the right in this case.

The "Half volte and change" (diagram) consists of a half volte and a straight line on which the horse is led at an angle of forty-five degrees back to the wall where his posi-

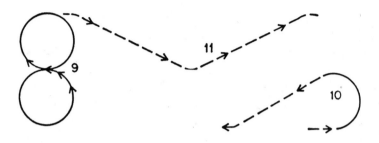

9. Figure of eight; 10. Half volte and change; 11. From the wall to the wall

tion is changed. This exercise may be begun in a corner or at any other point of the track. On principle this exercise must begin and end on the same wall.

Upon the command "Change direction from the center line" (diagram) the horse is turned from the short side of the school down the center and after a horse's length taken on a single track to the center of the long side where his position is changed.

"Serpentines along the wall" (diagram) may be ridden as single ones (one loop) or double ones (two loops). For the single serpentine along the wall, the horse, having passed the second corner of the short side, is taken on a single track approximately five meters away from the wall, describing a flat arc. At the point of half the school, his position is changed and he is taken back in the same manner to the same wall, reaching it before the corner to the short side.

When executing the double serpentine alongside the wall, the curve of the single one is repeated but the horse does not move away from the wall for more than three meters. The point of the exercise is that both arcs must be of the same size and that the horse remains on a single track.

"Serpentines through the arena" (diagram) may be ex-

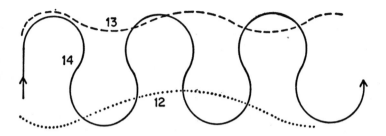

12. Single serpentine along the wall; 13. Double serpentine along the wall; 14. Serpentine through the arena

ecuted in three or five loops. The exercise starts either from the center of the short side or after the second corner of this side and comes to an end again in the center of the opposite short side or before the corner to this side. There are two different opinions in the world of dressage about the beginning and the end of this exercise. The importance with both remains, however, that all loops are of the same size and shape and that the horse remains on a single track.

In addition to the figures on a single track mentioned so far, those on two tracks, that is, lateral work, are practiced. Exercises on two tracks were minutely explained on page 109, "Dressage on a school horse." Here we enumerate only those figures which belong in the scope of this book. A complete list of exercises on two tracks may be found in *The Complete Training of Horse and Rider*.

In a "Half volte and change in the half pass" (diagram) the horse is made to perform a half volte on the single track and is then led back to the wall at an angle of forty-five degrees at the half pass.

For the "Half pass from the center line" (diagram) the horse is taken away from the center of the short side on a single track as if he were to perform "Down the center line."

After a horse's length on the center line, he is ridden at the half pass to the center of the long side, where his position is changed. He continues on a single track along the wall.

15. Half volte and change in the half pass; 16. Half pass from the center line

It is important with both exercises on two tracks that the horse be slightly bent and positioned into the direction of his movement, that is, he looks where he is going. His body must be parallel to the long side of the school, but the inside shoulder must be taken slightly into the direction of the movement. It is a fault when the hind quarters precede the forehand, which proves that the horse moves more to the side than forward.

The figures and exercises listed here offer an abundant choice of possibilities and combinations to the thinking rider and teacher, allowing the latter to compose interesting programs for his pupils at different levels without ever risking deviation from the principles of classical riding by trying to invent exercises of his own.

5

OVERCOMING DIFFICULTIES
AND SETBACKS

In the previous sections the progressive method of training was discussed and explained in detail. The present chapter is a summary of advice and directions for the teacher
in case of difficulties and setbacks, although some of them
have been mentioned in the course of this book. It is of
primary importance that the teacher, by constantly observing
horse and rider, become aware of any setbacks in time. If a
fault has gone unnoticed for a while, not only does its elimi-
nation become more time-consuming but also it will be increasingly difficult to detect the cause and thus find the means
of correction.

The teacher should remember that the cause of failure
may lie with the horse as well as with the rider, or often with
both. Furthermore, it may have its origin in both physical
and mental factors. Keen observation and rich experience
help to find the cause. There is more to riding than physical
skill, namely, mental agility and psychological insight which

enable the teacher and the rider to put themselves in the place of another creature, especially a horse.

With a horse, the psychological factors play a larger role than is generally assumed. Detecting the psychological origin of a fault will be easier for a teacher who has taken the trouble to ride his pupil's horse, a possibility, or, better, necessity, that has been repeatedly stressed. An experienced teacher remembers how often he had to revise an opinion derived from observation after himself mounting his pupil's horse. In this case it is also easier for him to understand his pupil and appraise and advise him in psychological respects.

The main difficulties with a horse lie either in his extreme sensitiveness or in his laziness and inertia—two entirely different motivations which demand the very opposite corrections. High-spirited animals, as we find among highly bred horses, often have a tendency to hurry, to rush off and even bolt because their natural reaction is flight. They become nervous with any change in their surroundings and react with different behavior to a new rider who has not yet found out how to deal with them. Fits of temperament in various degrees often occur with such horses. Younger ones, especially, take advantage of inexperienced riders to evade their rather vague influence by bucking, shying, or bolting. With such horses, calmness and patience are strongly recommended. They are to be given sufficient work without, however, exceeding their capabilities. Moreover, the riding teacher should interfere actively and ride the horse frequently in order to penetrate and understand his character and mentality and pass on his advice to his pupil.

Opposite in character and behavior are horses who lack any urge to go forward and whose sluggishness becomes obvious in their indifference to the rider's aids and encouragements. In one respect they are easier to ride for a beginner who is to learn the correct seat because there are no abrupt movements. But it is necessary for the teacher to interfere with the longe whip. If he doesn't, the student may easily acquire bad habits such as leaning back, constantly tapping with his legs, or assuming a poor position in the saddle. A horse's laziness is a serious impediment to progress in the training. Considering these factors, the training must be organized in such a way that the impulsion present in a highly bred horse must be controlled, while in a sluggish one it must be built up by riding him forward energetically.

Difficulties may also be caused by physical factors, though these may be avoided by choosing carefully from the large number of well-bred riding horses. A long weak back is a serious impediment because the horse often carries his head too high, dropping his back, which makes it difficult and painful for him to carry a rider and equally uncomfortable for the rider to sit. Progress in training is difficult to obtain and often does not exceed a certain degree. The problems with horses with weak hind quarters may be eliminated to a certain amount by correct gymnastic training, but they will always remain a weak spot. In both cases the teacher must remember that these horses tire more easily than others and have to be worked in shorter periods. Among the physical causes of difficulties we count the sensitive mouth of most high-spirited horses, which necessitates an especially light guidance and the use of bits with a very mild effect.

The cause of difficulties is not always or exclusively to be sought with the horse but in many cases is to be found with the rider or in the collaboration of both creatures. The behavior of the rider is more often than not the cause of problems. When he is unable to maintain a correct seat in the saddle, he misuses his aids to restore his lost balance. Instead of pushing his horse forward, he uses his legs to maintain his seat and holds on to the reins instead of guiding the horse. Sliding about in the saddle not only destroys any weight aids but also unbalances a young horse and even irritates a well-trained one.

Mental factors, too, are to be considered with a rider who, for instance, has had several falls and has lost confidence in the horse and in his own abilities. A horse feels any wavering or uncertainty in his rider and immediately takes advantage of it. Here, the only way of correction is the consolidation of the seat, which is best achieved on the longe.

The collaboration of horse and rider is the final possible source of failure to be discussed. In former times any experienced riding instructor of an important riding school was bent upon matching his pupils to his horses in a psychological way so that their characters complemented each other. It has proved advantageous to select a calm rider for a temperamental horse and a nervous one for a placid animal, thereby obtaining a certain harmony of characters. A phlegmatic rider on a quiet horse would soon fall asleep, while the combination of a high-strung rider on a nervous horse often leads to unexpected explosions. Those teachers could make exchanges when horse and rider did not comply with each other.

The situation being entirely different nowadays, such changes of horses and riders are rarely possible for the teacher. This confronts the instructor with the additional task of building up the mutual confidence and understanding between horse and rider, which is not only more time-consuming but also makes it necessary for the teacher to learn more about the horse by riding him himself. The pupil, following his teacher's example, should honestly try to overcome any dislike or aversion toward his four-legged partner. In most cases, the horse, too, may be induced by patient understanding to abandon any distrust of his rider.

After these general observations, the various difficulties will be discussed in logical order, following the course of a riding lesson.

It was said repeatedly that the horse must stand still during mounting and reasons were given for this requirement. It is demanded in dressage tests and belongs to the elementary training of a horse. It is especially important when the rider mounts alone with no one to hold his horse. However, it often happens that the horse begins to move as soon as the rider touches the saddle and does not wait for the command of his rider. This fault is more serious than may appear at first sight. Very often it is caused by the rider dumping his whole weight into the saddle. The horse reacts to the unexpected load of one hundred and thirty (and often many more) pounds by dropping his back. He throws his head up and begins to fidget, especially if he is a high-spirited creature. With a horse that has been raced it may be that he tries to rush off as soon as he feels the rider on his back. The riding teacher must interfere immediately but not by shouting or punishing the horse, rather by calming him with his voice and holding him by the cheekpiece or the reins. He should, however, avoid holding him tightly, which may frighten a nervous horse and provoke violent reactions such as rearing. The best way to induce a horse to stand still during mounting is by short elastic actions on the reins. The teacher must insist that the pupil lower himself gently into the saddle. The horse should stretch his neck with a low head, which may be taught to a young horse by feeding him sugar with the hand held low while the rider mounts. It is much easier for the horse to carry the rider's weight when in motion than at the halt. The experienced teacher asks the pupil to set the horse in motion before the horse begins to move on his own. With a young horse the duration of the halt should be gradually lengthened as the training progresses. All this might seem negligible to an inexperienced beginner but is very important to the education of horse and rider. The horse will soon realize that if he maintains a long neck and an arched back it will be much easier for him to carry the rider.

As we've seen in the chapters on training, as a rule the riding lesson begins with walk on the loose rein with good long strides which allows the student to adjust his seat to the movements of the horse while the horse may calmly take in the school and the surroundings. Meanwhile, the teacher observes horse and rider and decides the appropriate measure of work, which is especially important after days of rest or in a different place. The program of work depends also on the behavior of the horse and whether he is the phlegmatic or excitable type. He should not try to evade concentrating on work by giving way to playfulness.

This walk on the loose rein is a good introduction to work as long as the horse moves calmly with a long neck and a low head. Should he raise his head and begin to advance with short steps or show signs of playfulness, the teacher advises his pupil to try to induce the horse to stretch his neck long and low by a unilateral action of the rein on the stiff side. A short action on the very long rein turns the horse's head to this side and then ceases immediately. Generally the horse responds by lowering his head and stretching his neck. If he does not, the student tries the same aid on the rein of the other side. If there is still no result, the teacher orders the pupil to take up both reins and ride the horse forward at a rising trot, even foregoing momentarily the correct contact with the bit. Should the horse begin to hurry or try to rush off or buck, the teacher must warn his pupil by a short order to prevent a fall. "Take your body back!" works wonders in such a case. Also the instructor calms the horse with his voice.

In the beginning of this book I have pointed out the negative effect of a fall on the training of a beginner. The confidence of the rider in his horse and in himself is shaken and the horse realizes how easily he can evade the influence of his rider. However, should a rider happen to fall he must remount immediately. Some horses come to a halt after a rider falls. Others caper about and must be slowly herded into a corner of the school while the teacher talks soothingly to them. The pupil helps his teacher by also talking to the horse and avoiding any sudden movement which might frighten him. When this incident occurs during the lesson in a group, the other riders come to a halt immediately. As a rule the horse tries to join his companions and may easily be cornered. When the rider again has control over his horse, he must on no account punish him. If this incident happened because the horse shied away from something, the rider should lead him up to the object of his fear, show it to him, while talking and caressing him, and again approach the object and reassure the horse after having mounted. In any case, such an incident proves that quite obviously the rider's seat lacks firmness and that his guidance is still uncertain. Furthermore, it may be advisable to longe a fresh and gay horse for ten minutes before mounting to give him the opportunity to work off his friskiness. In case of a serious accident, the instructor calls for the help of a groom to take care of the horse while he remains with his pupil for whom he is responsible until he can hand him over to a doctor. Knowledge about first aid should belong to the mental equipment of a conscientious riding teacher.

The basic cause of most difficulties and setbacks is a faulty contact on the bit or its total absence. A horse taking a correct contact with the bit proves his obedience and his confidence in his rider. Contact was discussed in detail on pages 78–81 and 113. The rider can only guide his horse, especially a sensitive one, correctly, when there is correct contact on the bit, that is, when it is the horse that seeks the connection with the hand of his rider. I want to emphasize that the horse is not necessarily collected when he takes contact on the bit. There is no contact when the horse carries his head and neck high and comes above the bit, or when he overbends his neck so that his head comes behind the vertical line and he goes behind the bit. In both cases, guidance is made difficult for the rider. Moreover, the horse does not move in balance and the rider cannot sit correctly. Should the horse go above the bit, which often happens with excitable animals, side reins may be used temporarily to re-establish the contact the horse learned before under a more accomplished rider. This does not, however, eliminate the cause of the fault, which lies in the hand of the pupil. The rider's seat must be corrected and consolidated, which is best obtained by interspersing a short period of training on the longe. Sitting firmly in the saddle, the rider will not hold on to the reins. Sometimes a teacher resorts to a remedy that is absolutely and categorically to be rejected: he tries to force the horse to take contact with the bit by fitting the side reins extremely tight or, still worse, by using a running rein.

When a young horse goes above the bit, the cause is often pain in the back which might eventually lead to disobedience and resistance. This is a warning to the teacher that the horse is not yet strong enough to carry a rider in balance and that the pupil did not proceed with the necessary precaution and gentleness when mounting. This horse should have another series of longeing lessons in which he is taught to move with a low head and arched back. And the pupil must be reminded to lower himself into the saddle with utmost care.

If the horse throws his head up, evading the contact with the bit, the cause may not lie exclusively with the rider. The bit may be placed too high in the horse's mouth, causing pain, or it may be too narrow or too severe. But the hard hand of the rider may also cause the horse to throw his head up. The same causes may provoke an open mouth or difficulties with the tongue. If the teacher or rider neglects to eliminate the cause of these troubles in time, these bad habits are likely to become second nature to the horse and will take much more patience, skill, and time to be eradicated. Using forceful methods will never lead to success.

First the bit and its position in the mouth must be checked and the noseband tightened, but just so much that the horse can take sugar from the flat of the rider's hand. The teacher should direct his attention especially to the rider's hands, which should remain light and flexible. We speak about difficulties with the tongue when the horse hangs his tongue out on one side or places it over the bit instead of using it as a cushion preventing the bit of the curb or snaffle to press on the toothless bars of his jaw. The horse may also try to press his tongue between the front teeth, which counts among the grave faults. These difficulties, as we've seen, are entirely the rider's fault and correcting the position of the bit alone is no remedy, especially when these faults have become established habits. Some riders try to fix the tongue in the mouth with a tongue strap or a string (which is less noticeable to the observer but even more painful for the horse), but even if used currently by noted riders, this is again no remedy. Any violent measure is to be absolutely rejected.

It takes great patience and much sensitiveness on the part of the rider to cure a horse of difficulties with the tongue. In most cases the horse puts his tongue out to the side on which he takes a strong contact with the bit, leaning on the reins. He places the tongue under the bit to relieve its pressure on the bars. If, for instance, the horse puts his tongue out to the right, on which side also the bit of the snaffle is likely to protrude, the student gives a short but gentle action on the rein of the left (hollow) side to bring the bit in to its original position. Then he immediately applies the left rein while administering short half halts on the stiff (right) side. This exercise should be repeated in the course of the lesson, at the halt at first, which is easiest for the pupil who may concentrate entirely on his rein aids. Then the correction is carried out at the walk and later at the trot. In this pace the student pushes the horse forward with both legs to prevent the pace from slackening. As soon as the correction leads to even temporary success, the horse must be rewarded immediately so that he understands his rider. At the same time, the steady even contact on both reins must be cultivated, with care to push the horse forward sufficiently to maintain the fluent motion. Constant control and much patience are necessary until the horse forgets this bad habit.

The rider does not easily notice when his horse presses his tongue between the front teeth. The teacher, however, must detect this fault immediately. This habit occurs frequently in a nervous horse with a tendency to play with his tongue. As a correction, the noseband is tightened and the horse's attention must be kept awake by frequent changes of pace and speed and by performing different exercises during the lesson. The teacher should not neglect to watch the horse's mouth during training.

One of the most serious faults, which is severely penalized in a test, is for the horse to pull his tongue up and place it over the bit. This habit interferes with the correct contact with the bit and does not allow the action of the rein to go through the body of the horse and exercise the correct influence on the hind legs. To an expert observer, this fault is noticeable in all movements of the horse and is unmistakable proof of the heavy hand of the rider as well as of forceful methods of training. As a remedy, the bit is placed higher in the horse's mouth to prevent him from pulling his tongue from under it. However, it should not be placed so high that it pulls up the corners of the horse's mouth. Simultaneously, the instructor must return to the early stages of training and teach the horse to take a correct and steady contact with the bit. The pupil should be aware of the fact that he himself has caused this fault. The teacher centers his special attention on his independent seat and the lightness of his hands.

The instructor should never forget the mutual relationship between horse and rider. The rider's faults in seat and guidance are reflected in the movements of the horse, while shortcomings of the horse's training make it difficult for the rider to sit and perform exercises correctly. An Austrian cavalry inspector used to maintain that he concluded from the correct seat of the soldiers the degree of training of the horses and vice versa as he deduced from their action whether the riders applied the aids correctly.

Speaking of the rider's seat, I want to emphasize once again that the best way to eradicate particularly inveterate habits is to demand the extreme opposite in order eventually to obtain the correct result. A crooked stick is bent strongly into the opposite direction to make it straight. The teacher would, for instance, command his pupil to place his legs farther back if the rider had a tendency to stretch his legs too much to the front. As soon as he concentrates on some other things, his legs are sure to some forward again until they will finally remain in the correct place. When the pupil finds it difficult to erase this habit, the following exercise will help: the rider places the flat part of the thighs firmly against the flaps of the saddle, straightens his upper part, and stretches his arms straight down, his hands touching the heels which come up horizontally. The legs are bent in the knee, which must remain in place. By straightening the upper part and pulling the shoulders back, a hunched position is corrected at the same time. In the same way the teacher must correct most faults in the rider's seat and position. Consequently, a pupil who leans back, sitting as in a chair, is made to take his upper part forward and stretch his legs with a low heel as long as possible while the flat part of the thighs remain firmly against the saddle. Another who tilts forward, sitting on his fork, is ordered to take his upright body back in an increased measure, shift his weight firmly onto the seat bones, and take his legs forward, placing the knees against the flaps of the saddle. Here is a helpful exercise: the pupil remains in the saddle as just described and alternately lifts the knee until the thigh is parallel to the horse's back, the angle of the thigh to the lower leg decreasing. The pupil must remain in balance with his seat bones firmly in the saddle and must not slide or hop about on the horse's back. When a pupil clamps his calves to the horse's sides, losing the firm grip of the knee, he is asked to turn his thighs extremely flat against the saddle from the hip down, even pulling his riding breeches and thigh muscles forward with his hands while the knees are firmly applied to the saddle and the toes turned inward against the horse's body.

When correcting the seat, the teacher should at the same time control the length of the reins. If they are too long, the pupil is induced to lean back or stick his elbows out. Remember that the rider's arms are supposed to be held close to the body and not stuck out like the handles of a pot.

Let us go back again to the contact with the bit, which is obtained gradually in the course of the training and depends on the disposition of the horse and on the skill of the rider. It helps the horse to find his balance and improves his confidence in the rider. From the simplest demands made on a riding horse up to the most difficult exercises, the contact with the bit plays an important role. It leads up to the correct position of the horse's head and is a basic element of collection.

A horse evades the desired contact with the bit by throwing his head up, going above the bit, and not following the action of the rein. As a consequence, he drops his back.

Most nervous horses have this tendency, and, because carrying the rider becomes difficult in this position, their nervousness increases. These horses easily go out of control; they lose their balance and hurry along with irregular, hasty steps. To bring these horses along in their training calls for a skilled rider with a quiet temperament and a light hand. A horse is said to hurry when his steps become faster with the increase of speed but not longer, as they should. Hastiness becomes particularly obvious at the walk and trot but is also noticeable at the canter. It would be a mistake to push such a horse forward energetically, which would make the sequence of his steps even faster without making them longer. The rider should try to make his horse relax by trotting him with short supple steps on a long rein at the sitting trot. This exercise has a calming effect both physically and mentally and helps an excited horse to find the regular rhythm of his steps. When this result is obtained, the rider applies the reins very lightly and rides the working trot, and after a while, the ordinary rising trot while observing strictly the regular rhythm of the movement. Only then may he try by cautious pushing aids to make the horse lengthen his stride. Should he relapse into his habit of performing hasty, irregular steps—a sure sign that the stride has not lengthened—the rider resorts immediately to the short, loosening trot. By following this line consistently, the rider teaches his horse to move correctly. And it offers the best opportunity for the instructor to teach his inexperienced pupil the true rhythm of the horse's movement and to develop his feeling for it.

Difficulties of a different kind may be expected with a horse that is overbent. He evades the rider's influence by coming behind the bit. He is reluctant to go forward and often becomes resistant. This habit is the product of faulty training as well as of the heavy hands of the rider. The lack of forward urge becomes obvious if the horse does not react when the rider commands an increase of speed or the transition into a higher pace. Another form of reluctance to go forward may be seen in the hastiness of the steps which do not gain ground to the front upon the signal of the pushing aids. However, some breeds of horses with a high knee action naturally have this tendency, which must be taken into consideration during training. Such a horse can be made to lengthen his stride only very gradually and the trainer must be satisfied with the smallest progress. On the other hand, as soon as the horse responds to the pushing aids by performing hasty steps, the rider resorts immediately to the working or shortened trot until the horse has recovered the regular rhythm of his steps. Only then may he again try to obtain longer strides—a procedure similar to that used with a nervous horse.

In general, faulty contact is caused by faulty training. Neither a horse that goes above the bit nor one going behind the bit will be able to produce pure, natural paces. For a remedy, the horse is ridden forward with a long neck and a low head, as was practiced in the early stages of training. The rising trot alternating with very short periods at the sitting trot, just as when training a young horse, is the best way to make him forget his reluctance to go forward. Exercises in a collected speed, such as voltes and turns, should be avoided as long as the horse does not go forward freely. If this reluctance to go forward is recognized in time and corrected as just described, success will become obvious in the form of correct contact with the bit.

The picture changes when the horse has become conscious of how easily he can evade the rider's influence by his lack of forward urge. A clever and stubborn creature may develop this reluctance into complete resistance in the face of which the young rider is rather helpless. The horse refuses to advance; he creeps back or rises on his hind legs. Rearing or standing up on the hind legs in most cases is an act of despair when demands beyond his capabilities have been made upon the horse and reinforced by violent and rough methods—a very sad testimonial for rider and trainer!

Even this great difficulty should be met with patience and calmness. When a young horse shows the tendency to remain at a standstill or to creep back, he should be led on by the teacher or the groom holding him at the cheekpiece or by the reins. At the same time, the pupil gently applies both legs to the girth, cautiously reinforcing this pushing aid with the whip near the girth and giving a click of the tongue. When the horse is particularly stubborn, the teacher may help with the longe whip. Standing somewhat behind the horse, he lifts the whip and drops the lash to the ground. He may also touch the horse lightly behind the girth. On no account must he hit the horse with the longe whip, which might provoke even greater resistance and cause an accident to the pupil.

So far with the insubordinate horse punishments were avoided, but the situation is entirely different when the horse tries to evade the rider's influence by rearing on his hind legs. Now the rider leans his body back, holding the reins very lightly in the left hand. He may hold on to the pommel of the saddle with this hand. The right hand holding the whip administers a short energetic blow behind the girth. At this, as a rule, the horse leaps forward and the rider must not jerk him in the mouth with the reins. This drastic correction is the right answer to the horse's declaration of war and is usually sufficiently effective to prevent another attempt at insubordination. Merely raising the whip will make the horse leap forward the next time he tries to rear, and soon he will give up this bad habit. It goes without saying that the instructor must not expect this kind of correction to be administered by a beginner but should ask an experienced rider to carry it out or do it himself.

It is a typical sign of reluctance to go forward and of insubordination if the horse refuses to advance after the rider has mounted or when he comes to a standstill every time he passes the exit to the stables. Shying away from various objects which he has had sufficient opportunity to examine, if occurring repeatedly, may no longer be taken for fear but is plainly inattention, disobedience, and even resistance. Now the teacher strictly demands that the horse pass the object without altering his speed. At first the forward urge is cultivated by riding changes of speed, and the horse's obedience must be consolidated by performing turns and circles, halts, and moving on again. At a brisk trot the pupil rides as closely as possible past the object. If the horse tries to edge away to the right, for instance, he should not be pulled toward it with the left rein as an inexperienced rider might try. The horse would turn only his head to the left but sidle to the right with his whole body. In this case the rider increases the position of the horse's head to the opposite side, that is, to the right in this instance, and pushes him forward with both legs. The right leg is placed behind the girth to prevent the hind quarters from swinging to the right. The right rein is firmly applied and supports the preventive right leg.

In case of repeated insubordination and resistance, it is advantageous to retrain the horse on the longe for some time. He is made to go briskly forward at the trot with long good strides (not with hasty ones!) on a very large circle.

With high-strung horses, faulty contact may lead to yet another form of insubordination, which is bolting. Once and forever the teacher must make it clear to the pupil that a steady pull on the rein cannot, on any account, restrain a bolting horse. The relation of the rider's weight to that of the horse is at least one to eight or more, and the horse can out-pull his rider at any time. The only way to bring a bolting horse to reason is a taking and giving action of the reins—

especially when he pulls—and calming him with the voice at the same time. Shrieks will only make the horse the more excited. In order to apply this giving and taking action of the reins effectively, the rider needs an independent seat which once more is proved important. The rider is warned against jerking sharply on the reins to prevent his horse from bolting. Apart from the fact that such methods hardly succeed, the tension between horse and rider is increased, which is a serious impediment to profitable co-operation. When this incident occurs with a beginner, the teacher, who should be familiar with the habits of the horse, must interfere at the first attempt to bolt by giving short orders to the pupil. Often it is sufficient to perform a circle to bring a horse to reason. On the circle the pupil's influence is more effective, and a horse usually reduces speed. Calming the horse with the voice will be of help, as school horses generally react to the teacher's voice better than to that of the pupil. The pupil's seat may need consolidating, preferably by a few lessons on the longe.

One of the basic principles in riding is the axiom "Straight and forward." We've discussed the remedies to cure the lack of forward urge. Straightness is present in almost any horse when at liberty or ridden cross-country, that is, his hind legs move in the direction of the hoofprints of the forefeet. The situation is different in an indoor riding school or a fenced-in arena. Here crookedness may become a habit to the horse that leans with his shoulder toward the wall or the fence. This habit was already discussed in the chapters about training. It is of primary importance to eliminate this fault, because neglecting it would inevitably entail numerous other difficulties. The remedy was also explained in the chapters about training. The forehand is taken away from the wall and placed in front of the hind quarters. This will succeed only when the horse takes an even contact on both reins. If he does not, he increases the position of his head on his hollow side while his shoulder remains along the wall and his body becomes crooked. The rider should not be fooled by the increased position of his horse's head to the inside but look at the outside shoulder. An exaggerated position of the head acts like a brake to the horse's impulsion. Also he should be bent evenly from the poll to the tail and not flex his neck more than his body. When looking down, the rider should not get more than a glimpse of his horse's inside eye. Taking the horse out on a cross-country ride is the easiest remedy, as it teaches him to go well forward and move on long straight lines without being restricted in his movements as in an arena. However, not every rider has the chance to go cross-country and must correct his horse in the riding school. As with a young horse, the even and steady contact with the bit on both sides must be established in the first place. Riding parallel to the long side of the school or on the center line counteracts the horse's tendency to push his shoulder toward the wall and go crooked.

Work on the circle, however useful for the training of a riding horse, is of value only when carried out correctly, that is, when the horse is bent evenly from the poll to the tail according to the arc of the circle, with his hind feet stepping into or in the direction of the hoofprints of the front feet. It is important that the horse follow the same arc of the circle and does not alter it at will: increasing or decreasing the size, going on a straight line for a short distance, throwing his shoulder into the circle until he describes a many-sided figure instead of a circle. The teacher should remind his pupil to carry both hands closely side by side above the withers and keep his elbows along his body. Sticking the elbows out or leaning the upper part back means that the rider is guiding the horse with reins that are too long, which makes his hands unsteady and prevents the horse from taking an even contact.

When, for instance on the left rein, the horse swings his hind quarters to the outside, that is, instead of stepping into the hoofprints of the forefeet, the hind legs step to the outside of the circle, the rider may conclude that the horse makes himself stiff on the left and opposes the lateral flexion on this side. In this case it is above all important to establish the even contact on the bit by administering half halts on the left rein, that is, the stiff side. The right rein remains applied until the contact becomes lighter on the left side and the horse seeks the same support on the right rein without, however, taking an exaggerated position to this side, making himself hollow. He should remain in unaltered movement and on the same track of the circle.

A horse that swings his hind quarters to the outside when on the left rein is likely to adopt too much flexion on the right rein. He places his hind quarters into the circle and again the hind feet do not follow the hoofprints of the forelegs. His neck is bent more than the body, and he takes little or no contact on the right rein, making himself hollow. The rider pushes the horse forward energetically while holding the right rein applied and straightening the horse by short half halts on the left rein.

If flexed correctly from the poll to the tail according to the arc of the circle, the horse remains on the track describing a true circle when the pupil shifts his weight to the inside seat bone. The rider should not need to use the action of the rein to guide and direct his horse all the time, but by the position and flexion of his body the horse should be made to move on his own in the desired direction. When he falters and digresses from the prescribed line, the rider administers half halts on the rein of the side on which the horse makes himself stiff. At the same time he increases his leg aids and the influence of his weight because the forward movement must not be interrupted. When giving half halts on the inside rein, the pupil must be reminded to apply the outside leg behind the girth to prevent the hind quarters from swinging to the outside. The horse deviating from the circle reveals to the teacher his lack of suppleness. The actions of the reins do not pass through his body influencing his hind legs. Consequently, he loses his balance and becomes crooked. Here is an infallible test for the correct performance of a circle: when going large from the circle the horse must be able to go a straight line. If he is crooked, work on the circle was incorrect.

Since the crookedness of the horse becomes particularly obvious at the canter, care must be taken when striking off that the horse does not place his hind quarters to the inside at the moment of transition. In most cases the fault lies with the rider who uses his outside leg too strongly and too far behind the girth when commanding the strike-off and so pushes the hind quarters to the inside. The pupil should prepare his horse for the strike-off by giving him a slight position of shoulder-in and then demand the canter mainly with the inside leg on the girth. He shifts his weight onto the inside seat bone. It may happen that the horse responds to these different aids by striking off on the wrong leg. For correction the rider should proceed in the same way as when training a young horse. He should take him calmly into the trot again and repeat the exercise. On no account when these first attempts of a strike-off fail should the horse be punished by bringing him to an abrupt halt, as may be done with a fully trained but inattentive riding horse.

Inattentiveness toward the rider, which is very unpleasant with a jumper or when riding a dressage test, may best be counteracted by frequent changes of speed and pace. Thus the horse is obliged to concentrate on his rider and to try to understand the language of the aids. Besides, changes of speed and pace are excellent gymnastics for the improvement of suppleness and contact.

The correct position of the head is another detail that should be constantly controlled. Sometimes the rider is so much absorbed in his work that he does not notice that his horse tilts his head. This bad habit is mainly due to faulty contact with the bit, and when neglected for some time is the more difficult to eliminate. When looking down on his horse's head the pupil notices that one ear is held lower than the other. He straightens the head by giving short actions, with his hand held a little higher, on the rein on the side of the lower ear. This short giving and taking action is repeated in the course of the training until the horse straightens his head and both ears remain at the same level. The rider must not give a steady pull on the rein, which would induce the horse to lie on it.

Let us impress once more on the teacher that he should not demand any exercises without having first established the correct contact and position of the head. The correct position of the head is a step toward collection which, by the judiciously balanced influence of the pushing and the restraining aids, allows the gymnastic training of the horse by increasing the activity of the hind quarters.

We've stressed the importance of riding correctly through the corners of the riding school as a preparation for narrow turns and voltes. This rule is often misunderstood: the horse is taken into the corner in fact but with his head positioned to the outside, his hind quarters swinging to the outside, and with a loss of rhythm. Such a corner is of no value to the training. Similar faults occur with turns and voltes. Furthermore, at the trot and even more so at the canter the following faults appear for which the teacher should watch out in order to be able to teach the rider the necessary counteraction: the hind quarters swing to the outside, especially when there is no wall to prevent them from doing so; the hind quarters fall to the inside, especially at the canter, and the horse becomes crooked; he throws himself on his inside shoulder and comes out of control; when asked to turn down the center line or on a line parallel to the wall, he is unable to go a straight line.

If the hind quarters swing to the outside the influence of the outside rein and the outside leg must be increased. The teacher checks whether the rider's outside leg is placed sufficiently far behind the girth to assure the preventive effect. When the hind quarters fall to the inside, the pupil counteracts as with a crooked horse, that is, he takes the shoulder of the horse in with both reins. If the horse throws himself on his inside shoulder, the rider raises his hand holding the rein on this side for a moment without, however, forgetting to apply the rein on the outside at the same time.

It is easier to ride the horse straight along the track because the wall helps to maintain the direction. When turning across the school—from the long side to the opposite one (which is easier because of the shorter distance) or from one short side to the other (which is more difficult because of the longer line)—care must be taken that the horse does not begin to sway. As a preparation as well as correction, the teacher asks the pupil to ride parallel to the wall and at a distance away from it for a while as he sees whether the horse remains straight. By repeated changes of speed the forward urge is awakened and maintained while care is taken that the horse does not become crooked when reducing the speed. The teacher reminds the rider to take the horse's shoulder to the inside before reducing speed. Also, it is important that the rider carry his head upright and look straight over the ears of his horse into the direction to which he rides.

There is yet another detail teacher and pupil must not neglect when practicing turns. The horse should approach the opposite side on a straight line up to a distance of three steps from the track. He must not be allowed to turn on a larger arc following his own will or to edge to the outside to make work easier for himself. Anticipation must not be tolerated as it undermines the horse's obedience to the aids. As a remedy to such bad habits, which occur frequently with intelligent horses, the teacher commands the rider to change the rein when arriving on the opposite wall, announcing this order in time for the pupil to think about the different aids.

Anticipation of the rider's aids may become a habit when instruction follows a set pattern and when the exercises are practiced in the same sequence every day. After a while, most horses will no longer wait for the rider's aids. Also, they soon obey the teacher's familiar voice before the pupil applies the aids. Such over-eagerness of the horse must not be accepted for two good reasons: he evades the rider's influence and performs the exercise less precisely. With a horse anticipating the rider's aids the lesson should be made interesting by frequent changes of speed and pace, varying the exercises so that he does not know what comes next. A sensitive rider feels his horse's anticipation and performs the very opposite of what the horse was about to offer. When the instructor notices that the horse pays more attention to his voice than to the student's aids, he changes his commands and arranges with his pupil that, for instance, upon "trot" he strikes off into the canter and so forth, thus teaching the horse to concentrate on his rider.

When practicing a series of various exercises, the urge to go forward should not slacken. It becomes noticeable with the decreasing activity and flexion of the hind legs and the decreasing suppleness. This loss of impulsion must be made up for by riding changes of speed and pace or interspersing a period at a brisk ordinary canter, which changes the physical and mental indifference of the horse into alert attention and obedience.

In many riding establishments as well as in dressage tests in competitions, the observation may be made that most riders, even when participating in more advanced dressage classes, find it difficult to ride a correct volte of six steps' diameter. In most cases the voltes are too large, egg-shaped, or many-sided. They are often performed with the hind quarters swinging to the outside and do not give the impression of ease which may be expected from this apparently simple exercise. These variations point unmistakably to faulty collection and the lack of suppleness which do not allow the action of the rein to pass through the body of the horse. The teacher must eliminate these causes, for repeated practice of these incorrect voltes does not lead to any satisfactory result. Frequent changes of pace and speed, halts and move-off, large circles and turns with and without a change of rein, taking care that the horse remains in steady contact with the bit, eventually make him supple and flexible and enable him to perform correct voltes. It is advisable to increase the degree of difficulty gradually by first performing a large circle and by way of a larger volte of eight steps' diameter arrive at the volte of the prescribed size of six steps' diameter which, if executed correctly, is of great value for the gymnastic training of the horse. Stiffness on one side and exaggerated flexion on the other are the most frequent impediments to a correct volte. Therefore, the teacher should remind the pupil to establish even contact on both reins. When a horse begins to anticipate the rider's aids it is advisable to alternate voltes with serpentines or a half volte and change.

For the serpentine the rider performs a half circle on the left rein, for instance, and continues with a half circle on the right rein. With the number of half circles the degree of difficulty of this exercise increases as their size must decrease. Serpentines are executed correctly when all half circles are of the same dimensions and when the change from one rein to the other is performed in unaltered rhythm and with a supple change of the lateral flexion. In practice, most horses have an inclination to execute a smaller half circle to their stiff side. They are easier to turn to this side because of the firmer contact on the bit, but they move stiffly as they find the lateral flexion uncomfortable. On the other rein, to the hollow side, they evade the rider's guidance by exaggeratedly bending the neck. Often the hind quarters swing to the outside. By establishing an even contact on both reins the pupil counteracts the stiffness and also turns his attention to the crookedness of the horse which may frequently be observed in this case. When practicing serpentines the horse often anticipates the rider's aids and throws his shoulder into the half circle. Now the pupil continues the half circle into a complete volte instead of describing another half circle on the other rein.

Riding a figure of eight serves the same purpose as a serpentine. The figure of eight is easier when consisting of two large circles. When made of two voltes it is a more difficult exercise and should be demanded at a more advanced period, that is, when the pupil knows how to perform single voltes correctly. The important moment for the gymnastic training is the transition from one rein to the other and the simultaneous change of position and lateral bending. This exercise may also be used as a correction when the horse anticipates and tries automatically to perform circles and voltes.

The half volte and change permits the change of rein and helps to counteract the horse's anticipation of the rider's aids. Performed correctly this exercise is a test of the horse's obedience and his exact reaction to the aids. Often the observation may be made that on completion of the half volte the horse does not return to the wall straight and on a single track at an angle of forty-five degrees but throws his whole body in the new direction. This happens particularly often when the horse has learned the exercise "half volte and half pass." As a correction the rider does not take his horse back to the track after the half volte but rides him straight on parallel to the wall toward the short side of the school.

Many horses as well as riders find it difficult to perform a correct halt, especially from the canter. Either the halt is abrupt and on the forehand or the horse executes steps of walk or trot in between, or he comes to a crooked standstill and with his hind legs not under his body. I've explained the correct halt in detail in the chapters on training. The rider obtains an abrupt halt when he fails to collect his horse sufficiently before the exercise to make the hind legs step well under the body. A horse anticipating the rider's aids also performs an abrupt halt. In both cases it is advisable to practice changes of speed, the rider taking care that the horse remains straight and in correct collection, obeying the pushing aids of the legs. Then the rider merely braces his back while applying his legs and giving half halts to make the horse reduce the speed. An increase of the reducing aids —the legs pushing on the girth and repeated short half halts while bracing the back—makes the horse come to a standstill as demanded by the rules of classical equitation.

When the horse performs a crooked halt, swinging the hind quarters to the right, for instance, the rider's leg was ineffective on this side. The same method of correction as explained above is applied, while the leg on the side to which the horse becomes crooked is used with stronger influence. If the horse begins to anticipate the aids, especially when the rider thoughtlessly practices the exercise too often on the same spot, he is pushed forward energetically with both legs and the halt naturally demanded in a different place.

The difficulties enumerated above are caused mainly by a lack of impulsion and forward urge and are remedied by an increase of speed and changes of tempo. Those which may be traced back to a faulty balance, as, for instance, when the horse does not come to an immediate standstill but performs steps of walk or trot in between, should be corrected by cultivating the collection and making the hind legs step well under the body.

The rein-back, which for practical reasons must be expected from any riding horse, presents no problem provided the training has followed the rules of classical riding. The correctness of the execution may be considered a test of the degree of training both horse and rider have reached. The situation is different when severe faults or shortcuts were committed during the training or when forceful methods were applied. Then the horse leans on the rein and seeks support on the rider's hand. In this case the horse was collected from the front backward and may refuse to rein back altogether. His resistance may even lead to rearing and he may fall over backward. This is a perfect example of utter lack of suppleness and obedience. As so often during the training of horses and riders, the teacher must go back to the early stages and endeavor to make the horse forget his resistance. To begin with, the horse is made to step back two or three steps in the stables and with a halter and without the saddle. The same is demanded outside the school. As the next step, the teacher demands the rein-back without a rider but with saddle and bridle. The pupil stands in front of the horse, places his hands on either side on the rings of the snaffle, and makes him step back by giving alternate short actions on the reins. This procedure should take place at the end of work and the horse must be generously rewarded when obedient. Subsequently the pupil practices the rein-back when mounted, at first with the support of his teacher, who, as described above, reinforces the alternating rein aids of the rider. Later the rider practices on his own, and as a reward to make the horse understand, he dismounts immediately after. When the horse no longer leans on the rein the rider may demand the rein-back with both reins, as is the correct rule. At the same time, during the daily training the teacher directs his special attention to the correct contact with the bit. He controls the hands of the pupil as well as the influence of his seat which is of great importance with the rein-back. The rider can make stepping back easier for the horse by taking his upper part forward ever so slightly, without, however, lifting his seat from the saddle. Again the horse must be made to go forward briskly and in frequent changes of speed from the ordinary to the collected trot and vice versa as the correct collection, which is necessary for the rein-back, is practiced and consolidated. The experienced instructor demands not more than two to three steps backward in the beginning and does not increase the number of steps before these three are performed correctly.

The reader may have noticed that for almost all cases discussed in this chapter one of the remedies is the increased impulsion gained in changes of speed and pace. In the course of the entire training the teacher must bear in mind the overall aspect of instruction. For the training of horse and rider consists of numerous details which are closely related to each other. This is why, when trying to eradicate a fault or a difficulty, it is hardly ever constructive to practice the exercise in question repeatedly. The teacher should return to the early stages of training, for it is the faults in the basic schooling that cause the difficulties later on and make themselves felt in every exercise up to the airs of high school. Therefore, I want to impress upon the reader once again that the time devoted to the correct foundation of training is never wasted but helps to build a solid basis on which the more advanced exercises are accomplished with ease.

6

PARTICIPATION
IN COMPETITIONS

In all sports, competitions offer the opportunity to determine the standard reached. By measuring one's abilities against those of other competitors, progress or setbacks are registered, stimulus gained for further training, and the athlete's ambition spurred to increase his efforts. Besides, the athlete and his trainer gain experience which may be of value in their co-operation. In a word, competitions are the milestones in the career of an athlete.

These opportunities are provided by horse shows. In a classical sense, there are three main divisions in these events: dressage test; stadium jumping; and combined training, which consists of a dressage test, an endurance phase, and stadium jumping. It is intentional that the dressage test is placed first, for dressage alone lays the foundation on which the two other branches of the sport of riding may be successfully developed. This section will deal with dressage only, for details about competitions in jumping and combined training would go beyond the range of this book.

The word dressage for the training of the horse which aims at understanding this creature with all his strong and weak points and at shaping him in correct gymnastics is a somewhat unfortunate expression. It suggests a circus and one thinks of tricks, of drilling a poodle—in a word, performances that are the very opposite of what is expected of a riding horse according to the classical rules. However, the term dressage has become internationally used for this kind of riding and we must be resigned to it for, after all, it is not the name that matters but the manner in which to practice this sport.

The dressage of the horse—one might say the gymnastic schooling—beside implying a thorough study of the talents and shortcomings of this animal and the means of communication with him, aims at the cultivation of the movements he shows when at liberty or which he develops when correctly ridden. Dressage training, as we've said, lays the basis for all other branches of the sport. Therefore, it is not by chance but by a very wise decision that in many countries, the young riders must obtain permission to enter in jumping competitions by riding a dressage test of the first level. This spares the horse a great deal of wrong handling, prevents the ugly sight of riders fighting with their horses, and conveys to the young riders the correct approach to competitive sport.

Participating in dressage tests is highly desirable, provided that riding is taken seriously, because only then does this noble sport serve its purpose of physical and mental education. But there are those who ride only once or twice a week or on weekends and whose activity may not be called sufficiently consistent for competitive sport. Those riders should strive for a different aim, namely, to enjoy the hours of pleasure on horseback and content themselves with small progress in seat and guidance. If such a rider (or his teacher) gives way to the ambition to participate in competitions, he commits a grave mistake and does not do himself a good turn. He should remember that other athletes have to submit to severe discipline and be ready for great sacrifices for a chance to succeed. If he does not spend the time necessary for training, he should consider his riding as a pastime, limit his activities to pleasurable excursions, and remain a weekend rider. He should withstand the temptation to make his appearance on horseback in a competition. This well-meant advice does not, however, exclude presence at a horse show as a spectator. On the contrary, it is strongly recommended, for it should be interesting for every rider to see the result of consistent training of horse and rider. One can learn much by comparing performances, and the young rider is given the opportunity to distinguish good and faulty ones and to broaden his theoretical knowledge. However, utmost discretion and courtesy are recommended to the observer at horse shows. First, it may be that relatives of the criticized rider are standing nearby and overhear his remarks; and, secondly, experience has taught us that an expert, especially when a rider himself, takes a good and careful look before speaking his mind, while many a young or mediocre rider offers his criticism immediately as he tries to impress the other spectators. The knowledgeable bystander listening in silence to these effusions spots the greenhorn in no time.

As with many things in life, so with the sport of riding, success is not obtained by words but by actions. Consequently, teacher and pupil should not consider participation in a competition before the performance of horse and rider is at the level of the test. It is even strongly recommended that both achieve a considerably higher standard than demanded in this dressage class. When losing fifty percent of their capabilities, there should be sufficient left to allow the pupil to pass the test honorably. It is wise to calculate on such a high percentage in a horse show, for at a different place, with strange horses and unaccustomed and noisy surroundings, the horse is likely to be much less attentive and obedient than in the familiar ring. The rider, too, is excited and nervous, and exercises he accomplishes at home by the skin of his teeth will fail for sure in a competition. Therefore, the rider must have a perfect command of the exercises demanded in the program before even considering entering in a dressage test. Besides, the first appearance in ·public may be of decisive importance. In dressage, which is not judged by time or knockdowns, an initial failure may, in spite of the utmost impartiality of the judges, have an unfavorable effect on the reputation of horse and rider. A first start carefully prepared, on the other hand, makes an encouraging beginning to the future competitive career of a rider. The teacher should wisely curb his own ambition and that of his pupil and must not allow himself to be pushed by proud parents who very often cannot wait to admire their progeny at a horse show. By refusing, he chooses the lesser evil even at the risk of being reproached for preventing the child from collecting trophies. If the teacher is talked into sending his insufficiently prepared pupil to a dressage class and the young rider scores the lowest mark, the blame is usually laid on the judge, and parents, teacher, and pupil unite in protest against the verdict. The deeper meaning of riding remains entirely in the dark, that is, the educational value of teaching self-control and self-criticism.

The young rider's participation in a dressage class is decided by a board, so to speak, consisting of the teacher, the pupil, and the horse. In the course of the training, the instructor has sufficient opportunity to observe his pupil's progress and to deduce from his behavior whether he is qualified to appear in public. It is important to know whether the rider's seat is sufficiently firm, whether he has gained the experience and skill necessary to guide and influence his horse in different circumstances, and, above all, whether he has the ambition to measure his abilities with those of other riders. If from a feeling of insecurity he lacks this ambition, it would be very wrong to force him to participate, whoever may do the pushing, for it might entail a serious consequence: it might take away the pupil's pleasure in riding. The time that the pupil must devote to the preparation of a dressage test enters into consideration, too, for the young rider as well as for the advanced one. No athlete should enter a competition when he lacks the time necessary for training.

The pupil should seek his teacher's advice and verify conscientiously whether his physical as well as mental abilities are adequate to the demands of the various dressage classes. During the lessons and when discussing competition with his teacher, he has sufficient opportunity to get a clear picture of the degree of difficulty of the dressage tests and of his own weak and strong points.

It is more difficult with the third partner on the board, who lacks the gift of language. Here the knowledge of the horse's behavior and of his career must replace discussion. His age, the duration and quality of his training, and his temperament should be considered. Just as the rider should not enter a dressage test unless well prepared, so must the horse be up to the requirements of the class. A young horse should not appear at a horse show before having reached a certain standard of training, and an older one that has been ridden cross-country most of the time must first be prepared for the various classes. It is most rewarding for the pupil when he is able to enter in a test with his own horse that he has made himself and to whom he is certainly more attached than to a rented one.

15. Preparation of horse and rider for a dressage test

If upon mature consideration teacher and pupil have decided to start going into competition, and if the instructor thinks the horse suitable, his first duty is to introduce the pupil to the general rules. The International Equestrian Federation (F.E.I.), which was founded in the year 1912 when equestrian competitions were included in the program of the Olympic Games, has in the course of the years become the equestrian tribunal recognized by all countries. In the official rules of the F.E.I. the principles are laid down for the training of a riding horse and for the requirements made upon him. In concordance with those international regulations, the National Federations have issued their own rule books which differ from them only in negligible details. The knowledge of these regulations and their definition is of such great importance for the preparation of horse and rider for dressage tests that it is a vital part of the theoretical study of the subject. The importance of theory has, in any case, been repeatedly underlined.

The dressage tests are divided into different classes according to the degree of difficulty and the various stages of training. Tests of the First Level are intended for beginners, with the difficulties increasing with each higher level up to Level Four. Finally there are the three international dressage tests issued by the F.E.I., namely, the Prix St. Georges, the Intermediate, and the Grand Prix de Dressage, which is ridden at the Olympic Games. The present book is written for riders entering in the lower levels, while details for the advanced requirements of the higher classes may be found in *The Complete Training of Horse and Rider*.

The dressage tests of the lower levels call for a well-ridden horse going forward straight and with impulsion and with a regular rhythm in all his movements. By correct gymnastic training he should have been made to execute all turns and simple exercises with ease and harmony and submit calmly and willingly to the aids of his rider. This willing submission, which should convey the impression that it is the rider who thinks and the horse that executes the thoughts, makes riding a true pleasure.

These requirements were explained in detail in the sections on the training of horse and rider. Now it is a question of demonstrating these exercises in a fluent sequence in front of the judges who are to form an opinion in the time allowed for the test. For each class the organizer of the horse show may choose among a number of tests published by the Federations and the choice is made known to the riders in the announcement of the show. Without any doubt this makes it easier for the rider, who has an opportunity to make himself and his horse familiar with the test. On the other hand, there is the risk of drilling his horse to the test by riding it over and over again, mechanizing his horse to a certain degree, which is easily possible considering the long memory of the animal. This is, however, contrary to the idea of a dressage test. In the lower classes the program is usually read out by an announcer. Riding the tests by heart, as is often the custom in the English-speaking countries, burdens the rider's mind and diverts his attention, preventing him from concentrating entirely on his horse. The three tests of the F.E.I., however, must always be performed by heart.

As soon as the test is known, the teacher asks the pupil to ride the various exercises one by one, correcting faults and difficulties which are likely to appear as explained on pages 153ff, "Overcoming difficulties and setbacks." As the next step, it is advisable to practice parts of the test in the sequence in which they follow each other in the program.

This gives the instructor a good impression of the exercises when ridden in the prescribed order and reveals immediately which airs and figures need special attention and repeated practice. Moreover, the teacher can establish a schedule of work for the daily training. In the course of further practice, the complete test may be ridden at different times and faults immediately corrected. On no account should the complete tests be practiced day after day, for besides the possibility of mechanizing the horse, it would encourage the rider to become negligent about certain details.

Like a mosaic, a dressage test is made up of a multitude of items. First the tiny stones must be collected and organized. Then they are placed one next to the other and arranged in a certain order until eventually the pattern or the picture appears. In the same manner, the rider must first be able to perform the various exercises, executing longer sequences of the program as the training continues, until he is finally able to ride the entire program of the test. The teacher takes care that the pupil does not exceed the time allowed.

In the last phase of preparation for a dressage class, the teacher determines the exact time necessary for horse and rider to supple up and relax physically and mentally for the test. And this is of utmost importance for all classes, the elementary ones as well as the highest international competitions.

For any kind of sport, the correct "warming up" is an essential influence. The athlete must rid himself of any stiffness, loosen his muscles, and warm up his limbs. He must prepare himself mentally, concentrating entirely on the performance to come. It might be demonstrated graphically how in an upward curve he reaches the degree of elasticity and energy in which to give the best performance before having passed the zenith, when his capacity begins to decline again. In other branches of sport the trainer is able to find out the culminating point in discussions with his pupil. The riding teacher must draw his conclusions from the behavior of the horse. On the other hand, the inclination of the horse to cling to his habits helps to determine the duration of the period of warming up. When working at regular schedules, this lapse of time varies very little, so that an experienced rider as well as his teacher will soon know at what moment the horse is ready to perform. Beside the duration of time necessary for the preparation of a test, it is important to know the pace in which the horse supples up most conveniently. Both duration of time and pace vary with each horse. From the first moment of training the teacher should keep an eye on the watch when warming up, which will help him to have an exact notion of the required span of time when competition begins.

The best way to warm up is to begin with a quiet walk on the loose rein, moving around the area if possible to give the horse an opportunity to grow accustomed to different surroundings. When he has gone for some time with a good long stride, stretching his neck, the teacher asks the pupil to take up the reins and break into a trot. To start with he should ride a working trot with short loose steps and with the reins as long as possible. The hind legs must not drag but move energetically. The horse must seek the contact with the bit with a low head and a long neck. When he continues to maintain a steady contact with the reins correctly applied and moves with regular rhythm in the ordinary and collected trot sitting and rising, the teacher may conclude that this way of warming up has proved the correct one and times the approximate duration until this state of relaxation is reached.

If, however, the horse becomes nervous, going against the bit and with uneven steps, periods of walk in contact with the reins should be interspersed, from which the rider breaks quietly into the trot again, repeating the procedure several times until the horse maintains a quiet contact with the bit. When the horse loses his forward urge, changes of speed or the transition into the canter are advisable. After a period of canter there is generally much more impulsion in the trot. If the horse becomes excited by the canter, which is often the case in a strange place, the trot and even the walk are resorted to in order to regain the mental balance of the four-legged partner.

On rare occasions warming-up is done by riding a brisk ordinary rising trot immediately after mounting. But it should be remembered that, as an athlete would rather limber up by performing loosening exercises on the spot than by a sprint of several miles, so does a horse most likely tire by the ordinary trot as the beginning of work without, however, losing his tension and stiffness.

From the experience of the daily training, teacher and pupil decide by what exercises and in what lapse of time the horse is best prepared for a performance. After this preparation the teacher demands that the test be ridden without correcting possible faults immediately. This teaches the pupil to overcome any difficulties as discreetly as possible when they occur during the dressage class. After the completion of the test the faulty exercises are corrected independently, with the advantage of dismounting and sending the horse immediately to the stables when he has executed the exercises well. The period of warming up determined during the daily training is observed in the same manner before a dressage class.

At a horse show, even if well organized, it is not always possible to follow the exact schedule, and delays may occur which have to be considered when warming up. The period of warming up should not be too short or too long. But it is advisable to calculate the necessary time a little more generously than have it too short. In the first case and when there are delays in the schedule, periods of walk on the loose rein may be interspersed to prevent the horse from losing the briskness of his movements. It is most unpleasant, however, when the pupil is asked to enter the arena before he has had sufficient time to warm up his horse in the accustomed manner. The horse has not yet loosened up and does not concentrate on his rider, who is in a hurry and nervous and whose nervousness is transmitted to the horse. It is difficult to make a good impression on the judges in these unfavorable conditions.

I should like to conclude this chapter by reminding the instructor once again not to ask his pupil to ride the complete program of the test too often. An intelligent horse with his keen memory will try to anticipate the rider's aids in a short while and no longer perform the exercises in the correct manner. Constantly changing the sequence of the exercise best prevents this possibility during the preparation for the competition.

Furthermore, I want to impress on the young pupil and his parents that only one rider will win the class and that fair sportsmanship is best learned right from the beginning. Every competitor, however, should endeavor to prepare himself well enough for the dressage test to be sure to present himself and his horse honorably in front of the judges.

16. Rider and judge

Riding and judging are two subjects which at first glance seem to be intimately connected. In past years this relationship proved true in most cases at the various competitions. The rider and his teacher endeavored to perform to the best of their abilities, obeying the general regulations, and the judge, having justified his appointment by his equestrian knowledge both in theory and in practice, made his decision most conscientiously between the better and the less good competitors. The position of a judge in dressage, being based on the solid foundation of his knowledge, did not allow his decision to be questioned or criticized except on very rare occasions. The dressage riders gave proof of their self-control—developed by the sport of riding—and, bowing to the authority of the judge, submitted to the verdict without argument, much less protest. The judge did not derive his authority from his position but from the qualities of his character, his personality, and his knowledge.

I am fully conscious that I am approaching a delicate subject when I point out that the relationship between rider and judge has unfortunately changed a great deal in recent years. But this discussion would be of no use and I would lack the courage of my opinion if I did not call a spade a spade. Nowadays the majority of the riders and their teachers —the winner of a class excepted—have hundreds of arguments against the decision of the judges and never even think of their own and often very fundamental shortcomings. It happens that even the winner does not consider his marks high enough for his performance. These sorry phenomena so contrary to the deeper meaning of riding reach their climax when competitors, like dockers, go on strike against one or the other of the judges or make their participation in a show dependent on the choice of a judge on whose favor they are able to count. Does not such conduct convey the impression that rider and teacher on one side and the judge on the other are opponents while, on the contrary, they should aim at one and the same thing, namely, to preserve and promote the sport of riding?

Although there is no more cavalry or other form of military equitation which in former times constituted the main supporters of any equestrian activity, there is no doubt that the sport of riding has had an undreamed-of development in recent years. It is a fact that any sport practiced by the mass of the people is likely to present weaknesses in many respects. The larger number of riders, on the other hand, offers a greater possibility of detecting a truly talented and dedicated one and selecting him for further development.

An experienced and capable riding teacher generally has the capacity to act as a judge and give a correct and precise verdict. It should, however, not be necessary to point out that he must not judge a class in which his pupil takes part as a competitor. Furthermore, fairness and sportsmanship dictate that rider and trainer keep away from the judge on the show grounds before the competition and do not try to influence him in their favor. A conscientious judge is certainly willing, after the test, to explain or answer questions when there is any doubt about the descriptive comments which the judge has recorded for each competitor. Discipline and self-control gained in equestrian practice should, however, induce the rider to submit to the decision of the judge without grumbling. This chapter is meant to contribute to the understanding between rider and judge which is of utmost importance if the sport of dressage is to be continued in the future and is to find a growing number of disciples.

I have pointed out the necessary foundations for any kind of riding and especially for dressage. In this chapter the basic requirements made on a dressage horse which have been laid down in all rule books and, so to speak, represent the law to rider and judge are to be once more summarized. If horse and rider are both trained and judged according to this law, there should be no disagreement.

1. The horse should go forward straight and with impulsion.

2. The absolute purity of the paces and the regularity

of the steps should be maintained in all movements. It is this regularity that conveys brilliance to the dressage horse and is with reason called the music of riding.

3. The horse should remain on the bit calmly and confidently, seeking the rider's guidance and submitting willingly. The rider must never abuse by the reins to force the horse's head into a certain position. The visible lack of freedom in the horse's paces points immediately to this incorrect collection.

4. By appropriate gymnastics the horse is made supple and flexible, which becomes obvious in his smooth movements, fluent transitions, and, last but not least, in his absolute balance. This balance is possible only when the hind quarters are sufficiently active and carry a larger portion of the rider's weight.

5. The physical proficiency of the horse, which is the natural consequence of suppleness based on muscular control, and the presence of perfect balance are mirrored in the correctness of the exercises, in their exact performance as well as in the pure sequence of the steps.

6. The horse's obedience develops from his confidence in the rider, who must never demand more than the horse is physically able to do.

These basic principles must be clear to every rider and every judge, for the clarity of the concepts is essential to the development of any sport. The training of a horse must be free from mysteries—so much so that the methods are comprehensible to even an uninitiated onlooker even if he cannot apply them himself. The verdict of the judge should be equally free from mysteries although this has unfortunately not always been the case with judgments in recent years.

Nowadays the judge's duty is not only to give marks to the performances of the competitors and place them according to their standard but also he is expected to advise the rider and set up the guiding principles for his further work. The judge's record of the test plays an important role, for in it he lays down the reasons for his decision. As in a court of justice plausible reasons must be given for the conviction of the accused, so must the judge of a dressage class forego ruling like a dictator but in his annotated score or record explain his opinion. It should be taken for granted that in order to be able to fulfill his task the judge of a dressage class is or was capable of performing the test he is asked to judge, as is the case in most other branches of competitive sport. This is not to maintain, however, that every good rider is necessarily a good judge or, as was said before, a good riding instructor. Many a talented rider may bring his horse along with much sensitiveness and skill and reach an advanced level of training but is not capable of passing on his knowledge to a pupil or make use of it judging the standard of the performance of other riders. The situation is very delicate for a judge who, even though a rider, has never proved himself in a competition. How very difficult for him to give a line of conduct to the riders when he is unable to demonstrate the correctness of his opinion on horseback! This visible proof of his knowledge and understanding is as fundamental to the authority of a judge as it is for the reputation of a riding teacher. I prefer not to mention the judge who has never even been seen on horseback.

Every competitive sport is subject to discipline and when a group, a team, enters into competition there must be one of them or the trainer who as the leader assumes responsibility and insists that the others acknowledge his authority. In the sport of riding, which aims at the harmonious co-operation of two different creatures, horse and rider, authority and discipline are of even greater importance.

CONCLUSION

I have undertaken to write this book in a sincere endeavor to convey to the horse world and especially to young riders what practice has taught me in many decades. These pages were not dictated by theory but by my life in the saddle and by long years of experience with horses and riders. From the vast sphere of equitation I have tried to select the essential and most vital subjects related to the situation of teacher and pupil and to express myself as clearly as possible. Any problem that arises in the course of practicing equitation—the collaboration of two different living creatures —may be solved by correct and, more important, consistent education. Success depends on the knowledge and understanding of the teacher and the authority that emanates from his character and personality.

All my life I have believed that it is very important not to disappoint anybody. Therefore, I wish to pass on a piece of advice to the riding teacher: never promise more than you are able to deliver, and never demand more than your pupils—horse and rider—are able to accomplish. Much more important than any lofty ambitions is the teacher's task to make his pupil understand the feeling of responsibility a rider must have toward his horse and to impress upon him the guiding principle which must not be forgotten for the sake of exaggerated ambition and greed for ribbons: your horse should be your friend!

INDEX